bumping
into

God

again

bumping into God again

35 more stories
of finding Grace
in unexpected places

Dominic Grassi

LOYOLAPRESS.
A JESUIT MINISTRY
Chicago

LOYOLA PRESS.
A JESUIT MINISTRY

3441 N. Ashland Avenue
Chicago, Illinois 60657
(800) 621-1008
www.loyolapress.com

All Scripture quotations are from the Jerusalem Bible © 1966 by
Darton, Longman & Todd, Ltd., and Doubleday, a division of
Bantam Doubleday Dell, Inc. Reprinted by permission.

Some of the stories in this book appeared in a different version
in *Markings* Homily Service, published by the Thomas More
Association.

Cover design by Eileen Wagner
Cover art by Dennis Pryber
Author photo by Barbara Zeman
Interior design by Lisa Buckley

Library of Congress Cataloging-in-Publication Data
Grassi, Dominic.
    Bumping into God again : 35 more stories of finding grace
in unexpected places / Dominic Grassi.
        p. cm.
    ISBN 0-8294-1510-6
    1. Christian life—Catholic authors. 2. Grassi, Dominic.
I. Title.
    BX2350.2 .G696 2001
    242—dc21   00-060849

First paperback printing, January, 2003
paperback ISBN-13: 978-0-8294-1648-0; ISBN-10: 0-8294-1648-X

Printed in the United States
10 11 12 13 14 15 Versa 10 9 8 7 6 5 4 3

To my sister Annamaria.
Everyone needs an angel.

contents

introduction

IT SHOULD BE NO SURPRISE TO ME THAT THERE
is a second volume of stories about my "bumping
into God." After all, my life has continued as before,
as have my relationships and my ministry. Nothing
has changed dramatically. What has proved surprising to me, however, is that people not only read
the first volume but wanted more. I believe that's
because people are not so much attracted to my stories as they are pleasantly surprised to get in touch
with their own stories as they read mine.

Early in life, as I listened to my parents and
their peers, I learned what a privilege it is to be
able to share stories with others. I am still telling
my family's stories, and my friends—being good
friends—smile and nod agreeably as they listen for
the tenth time to something that I feel is as fresh
as Mom's homemade bread. I would guess that they
hear the enthusiasm in my voice and choose out
of kindness not to shut me down.

Now I find myself quite often introduced as
a "storyteller," and audiences actually sit in front of
me in rapt attention waiting for me to begin; they
want me to tell my stories. What a privilege! What

a gift! What a grace! What an opportunity for me to bump into God. I'm a lucky guy and I know it.

I am learning that stories beget more stories. For example, what sheer delight I felt when, during a question-and-answer session after a book reading, someone asked if the brother who was there in attendance happened to be the same brother who hid me in my stroller under a porch when I was a child, a story I recounted in my first book. He was indeed the one. Fifty years later I felt totally vindicated as he blushed and muttered that this was how I had immortalized him. How was it that at signings where my other brothers were present (brothers who were not the guilty ones) I was never asked that question? It was a moment to savor and became a new story to tell.

I'm also learning that there always seems to be a deep vein of stories left to mine. A person's memory is very much like a muscle. The more it is used, the better it will function. So we have more memories than we can immediately recall. At the same time, life goes on. And that provides us with additional opportunities and experiences. Our stories continue even as we are in the process of telling them.

Maybe all of this goes without saying. Of course our memories are full of untold stories, and of course we are making new memories and new stories every day as we go about ordinary life. But I am still finding it all amazing. My stories, as well as those of so many people I have encountered, have convinced me that God's presence is right here if only we take the time to reflect on it. Here is an example.

After a very difficult week, I really looked forward to turning the clock back at two A.M. on October 31, which happened to be Halloween morning. The extra hour of sleep would be just what I needed. For days prior I had found myself in the kind of deep funk that leads me to seriously doubt the existence of a hereafter, much less a God to go with it. That's a deep pit to fall into. The lethargy that followed would not even allow me to search for a sign. I was in no mood to bump into God. So God bumped into me, really hard. Should I have been surprised?

One would be tempted to say that in that "witching" hour when the clock gets set back and sixty minutes are repeated, time stands still. Isn't that a really good definition of eternity? And it was at that time, or in the lack of it, that I found myself walking down the street in the rain, rudely awakened from a deep sleep and a warm bed. I was on my way to a nursing home to anoint someone I had never met. I was locked out of the facility, and it took a lot of muttering and my trying four different doors before I could find a way to get in. Once there, I did my thing. I gave the dying woman and her grieving daughters a blessing and headed back home. I stepped back onto the street at exactly the time that all the neighborhood bars closed their doors. So the streets were now filled with costumed revelers. There was a Dorothy from *The Wizard of Oz* with very hairy legs and a mustache. I didn't want to walk too close to her. Or him? A doctor in his green scrubs high-fived me. In fact, people up and down the street were smiling at me. They did not see a priest. I was just another costumed partyer. I looked a little better than a guy I saw who had tried to dress as a priest; he was getting into a cab with his princess girlfriend.

I ran the rest of the way home, feeling totally out of place and uncomfortable. Once back, I tried to sleep, but I could not. In that one hour, that hour when time stood still, that hour that mirrored eternity, I had been given a choice. I could either do what I do, and do it well, trusting in God. Or I could just parade around, hollow and dressed in some costume that I had no right to wear. No, I didn't bump into God that night. God slammed right into me.

I realize that this introduction is starting to turn into a book of its own. It is very much like when Mom would set the table for unexpected guests, saying that she would just fix them up "a little something" to eat. Before you knew it, the guests and the table itself were moaning from so much food. And she would encourage them, saying "Mangia! Mangia! Eat! Enjoy!"

And so I say to you, "Mangia! Enjoy these stories!" But please, add some of your own. Tell them. Share them with others. Keep on bumping into God. And encourage others to join in with you. That is why I am offering these to you.

acknowledgments

LET ME TAKE THIS OPPORTUNITY TO THANK ALL the folks at Loyola Press and the incredible team they put together. I could not have felt such support and encouragement from any other group. Simply stated, they are remarkable. Their belief in what they are doing is infectious.

Barbara McNabb has the job of deciphering on a daily basis what I write even when I can't figure out my own scribbling. She continues to be a delight and incredibly patient.

My good friend and spiritual guide Ruby Alexander has heard every story, oftentimes over the phone, before anyone else has seen them. Her reaction indicates whether or not what I have written will see the light of day.

Mom and Dad, I always listened to your stories. Now I wish that I had listened better. What a legacy you have given to me.

My brothers have been not only a source of many of the stories I write but also a support in all that I do. They are special to me. Their encouragement means so much to me. I am grateful that they still put up with me. Come to think of it, maybe they do so because of the not-so-subtle threat of what I might write about them if they're not careful!

In fact, to all who know me: fair warning! You just may find yourself in these pages or, God willing, in some future volumes. I am always looking to bump into a good story, and into God in the process. Thanks for being a part of my story.

Stories of God's Patience

God's patience with us is in direct proportion to our
limitations, our silliness, and our sinfulness. How
ironic it is that we have tried so hard to surround
ourselves with labor-saving, energy-saving, and time-
saving devices and in the process have lost the skill
and art of being patient with ourselves. If God can
be so understanding of us, our challenge is to be

"Or again, what woman with ten drachmas would not, if she lost one, light a lamp and sweep out the house and search thoroughly till she found it? And then, when she had found it, call together her friends and neighbors? 'Rejoice with me,' she would say, 'I have found the drachma I lost.' In the same way, I tell you, there is rejoicing among the angels of God over one repentant sinner."

~ LUKE 15:8–10

---

accepting of the other

person, whether a scam artist, hoarder of toilet

paper, or wise bag lady. Fighting off a squadron of

fleas or sitting by a lake with a fishing pole in hand,

we have many opportunities to bump into God. We

need only be patient.

fishing

ONCE, ON A WARM SUMMER'S MORNING, MOM
shook my brother and me awake just as the sun was
barely brightening the eastern sky. It was too early,
but we did not even think of complaining as we did
when it was 6:30 A.M. and we were being dragged
from sleep to serve at early Mass. Toast, juice, bacon,
and eggs scrambled in olive oil were waiting for us
this morning. We tried not to look too excited as
we gulped down the food, but we were in a real
hurry. Once we finished eating, we gathered the
lunches Mom had packed for us, the worms we had
dug out of the backyard the day before, and the
minnows we had bought from Van's Bait Store on
Belmont Avenue. Lots of the minnows were belly-up,
but enough of them were still alive to guarantee
some fun.

While I picked up my bamboo pole with its
bobber and sinkers already attached to the line, my

brother Tony grabbed his trolley line and stringer and tackle box. Off we went to the rocks of Belmont Harbor, located between the Nike Missile Base, which protected us from a Russian sneak attack, and the Yacht Club, which protected the rich from the rest of us. We were ready for a full day of fishing.

I was a neophyte fisherman, my brother a veteran who took fishing seriously. Even back then he was a person of few words. Still, I could always tell when he was getting upset with me, like when I'd start playing with the minnows or forget to bait my hook correctly. Tony, who had a five-hook trolling line with a bell and spring attached that signaled when a fish was nibbling, would be all set up, baited, and in the water before I could get my simple three-piece pole prepared.

He'd start to catch perch right and left, determining which ones to save on the stringer line and which ones to throw back into the lake. Occasionally he would land a rock bass after a terrific fight. My brother always knew exactly what to do.

Not me, not by a long shot. It would finally get to Tony when, for instance, I'd keep pulling up the stringer to see if the fish he had caught were still alive. Eventually he would yell at me and I would get quiet and just sit there, bored and halfheartedly holding my pole. At those times I couldn't help but notice my brother watching the sun rise over the water and then leaning back and watching the clouds float by. I sensed that he was going off into his own world.

Later, when I was chasing a grasshopper instead of watching my pole, I got a bite that pulled the whole thing into the water. I panicked, not knowing what to do, until my brother calmly stepped onto the rocks and snagged it with one toss of a three-pronged hook. Unfortunately, it turned out that my catch was a fat garbage-eating carp that I wouldn't keep. My brother went back to calmly staring off into the distance. I grew even more bored, then very tired, and then hungry.

I broke open the sandwiches that Mom had prepared for us and wolfed down all of mine, not realizing it was only nine-thirty in the morning. My brother joined me, again without saying a word, just sitting there with one hand on the line and the other holding a peanut butter and jelly sandwich. Prudently, he saved half of his lunch for later. He knew it was only nine-thirty.

By 10:00 A.M., I had caught a few fish, lost even more along with a lot of the bait, eaten my entire lunch, chased some bugs, and become totally bored. Clearly it was time to go home. My day of fishing, in reality less than three hours, was over. But my brother would have none of that; he was going to stay.

Once I got home, I crawled into bed and slept for a few hours. After a real lunch at the right time, I went out in search of my friends, who I found playing in the alley, and joined them. It wasn't until after five o'clock in the evening that I noticed Tony walking slowly home. His face was beet red from the day in the sun and wind. The stringer thrown over his shoulder was filled with perch that Mom would reluctantly clean and then cook to perfection. Tony was a true fisherman.

In fact, he and another brother still are. On occasion, they will spend a vacation on the water. Fishing has developed into a real sport and hobby for them both. But not for me. I always needed more than just to sit there and wait for a fish to make its move. And that is really the shame of it. I haven't been fishing in decades, but something inside me believes that I'd enjoy it now. I'm just too embarrassed to learn how to do it.

I have a feeling that for my brothers and for a lot of other people who fish, one of the lures (no pun intended) of fishing is that once the line is in the water you have an excuse to sit and wait and do nothing else at all. Plus, you get to drink in the beautiful sights and sounds of the outdoors. Without the pole, there really is no excuse for just sitting there for so long a time. Only strange people sit and stare for hours on end.

What someone like me might call meditation or reflection or even prayer my brother simply calls fishing. Imagine how people would react if, on a warm day in the summer when the grass needed to be cut or the leaves needed to be cleaned out of the gutters, we said we were going down to the lake to stare or meditate or pray. They would think we were either lazy slackers or a little out of our minds. But if, instead, we pulled out an expensive, perfectly balanced, lightweight rod and reel and some exotic lures and announced that we were going fishing, people would quickly admire us for being so well-rounded and for having such a wholesome hobby.

Most of us could use a little time sitting, looking at the sun, feeling the breeze, and listening to the waves break on the shore. Fishing can be decidedly low-tech. It can be done while our thoughts melt into dreams and our hopes into intercessions. We can then find the quiet silence in the core of our heart and feel the great stillness that is there—indeed, the presence of God that is there. And if a fish happens to wake us out of that state, at least we will have something to show for how we spent the day.

toilet paper annie

I DON'T LIKE CHANGING NAMES IN MY STORIES, but I guess I will in this one. While I don't think "Annie" would mind if I properly identified her, others in her family would not sense my genuine affection for her and might become upset at me for making her story public.

I never knew Annie's husband. When I met her, he had been dead for a number of years, leaving her alone and frightened. It seems that her husband had taken care of everything—all the details, all the money, all the bills. Without any children to step in, Annie found herself left to deal with life on its terms and with no one to protect her.

Annie's husband had been a good provider. But despite the numerous insurance policies, the paid-off home mortgage, social security, and other bank accounts, Annie lived in dreadful fear that she would one day be broke and forced to live on the streets. So she began devising all sorts of ways to save her money.

To save on electric bills, Annie stopped turning on the lights and using appliances. Her brothers and sisters would come by her house and would sit with her in a living room that grew darker with every visit. Annie began to water down the wine she would serve them, and pretty soon it was only warm tap water in their glasses. Needless to say, they soon stopped coming by to visit.

Every Sunday, Annie would stand in church and run her hand over a plaque on which her husband's name was listed as a donor to the centennial campaign. Parishioners who felt sorry for her soon learned that any attempt at kindness, such as mowing her lawn, would evolve into a daylong commitment; she would beg to also have her windows washed, screens put in, and so forth, with never an offer of compensation or thanks.

Annie had an absolutely incredible knack for knowing when the church was having a function that involved food. With her large, sad eyes she would beg and beg until whoever was in charge of the event would let her in. It could be a thank-you party for festival workers, a cake and ice cream party after First Communion, even the Men's Holy Name Society Christmas Party. There would be Annie, filling her plate, her mouth, and her purse simultaneously.

Nothing was safe. Food, condiments, paper plates, and utensils would make it into her pockets. A few people would shake their heads self-righteously. But most did not begrudge her what would probably be her sole meal for a day or two. They were kind and patient with her. And this was fortunate for Annie. Some helping agencies in the area had banned her because she was so quick to pocket anything and everything.

Once, Annie joined a group of parishioners who went caroling on a cold December night the week before Christmas. The music director had kindly given her a small handbell to ring during the singing. Annie had a marvelous time. She endured the cold because the caroling would end with cookies and hot cocoa at a parishioner's house. When we got there, the food had not yet been put out, so Annie began to literally stamp her feet in anticipation. She suddenly spied a cut crystal bowl filled with exquisite looking hard candies. With a lightning grab, she had put three of them in her mouth before the shocked and frightened hostess screamed out from across the room that they were not candies. They were Italian glass pieces made to look like candies. Her husband had just brought them back from Italy. Annie quickly spat them back into the bowl. We never knew what the hostess did with them after the carolers left. But she did make sure that Annie went home with a shopping bag full of real sweets.

I'll tell you how Annie got her nickname. Every Sunday morning the bingo workers would come to me and complain that there had been no toilet paper in the women's washroom in the parish hall. This happened week after week. And week after week the janitor was blamed for not doing his job. And week after week the janitor insisted that on Friday afternoon the last thing he did before going home for the weekend was put a roll of toilet paper in each stall and an extra roll next to it.

Early one Sunday morning before the hall was opened for bingo, I checked. And I saw that there was indeed enough toilet paper to satisfy the needs of a small town for a week. So I waited for the hall doors to be opened for bingo. Sure enough, Annie was the very first one to come in, wearing her tattered red cloth coat flat at her sides. I watched as she walked into the bathroom and then came out five minutes later, her coat bulging as if she had just gained a hundred pounds. I sent someone in to check the women's bathroom. Not a sheet of toilet paper was left. Mystery solved and nickname given: "toilet paper Annie." It stayed with her until her death a few years later.

I wonder what her family found in Annie's home after she died. It was so sad that she wasn't able to enjoy what she did have. Sometimes I wonder what more we could have done for her. But her family got angry when anyone tried to help her, suggesting darkly that everyone was always after Annie's money. And that just wasn't the case.

At Annie's wake, as I looked at her tiny body at rest in the coffin, I was sorely tempted to get a roll of industrial-strength toilet paper and tuck it in the corner of the casket for her trip home, not to make fun of Annie, but as a reminder to God of how patient and kind most people had tried to be to this poor, sad lady. It's not that God needed a reminder to be patient with her. I suppose it would have been a way to let God know that we all loved Annie. We knew that now she was at peace as she was welcomed patiently into God's loving embrace.

i'll never know

I NOTICED HIM CRYING IN CHURCH. IT'S NOT
uncommon to find people crying in church. They
bring their sorrows and their frustrations, their fears
and their confusion, and place them before their God
in a sacred place, a place to which countless prayers
like their own have been brought over many years.
So I can usually handle that sight, unless it is a young
adult crying. Then it really bothers me. Quite honestly,
I feel that babies, children, and the elderly all have
more to cry about. When it is a young person who is
in tears, it usually means that a turning point or a life-
changing event or a shattered relationship has forced
him or her to face his or her own mortality, most
likely for the first time. Those necessary but painful
moments I find very hard to encounter in others.
I mourn the loss of innocence that the tears reflect.

So I could not help but see the young man sitting in the church, head in hand, long after the service

was over and the people had gone home. My experience taught me to be cautious and not to approach him unless he indicated that he wanted to talk. Quite often the person's struggle is solitary and would not be helped by any kind of outside intrusion.

I had started, instead, to set up the sanctuary for the next liturgy when I noticed that he had gotten up and was walking toward me. He was more informally dressed than most would be even these days, more for Saturday night than for Sunday morning churchgoing. His jeans were clean and pressed, his athletic shoes still white from their newness. He asked if we could talk privately. I said we could. He looked around to make sure we wouldn't be overheard or interrupted. With the next service only ten minutes away, I could only give him a few moments.

He began to tell me his story. He said that he had been diagnosed the day before as HIV positive. Upon hearing about it, his father had kicked him out of the house, calling him all sorts of crude names. While the young man admitted having numerous female sexual partners, he insisted that he didn't have a clue as to how he caught the disease. Locked out of his home, he had wandered around all night before finally crashing at a friend's house. It was cold, he reminded me, very cold. What he needed from me was train fare to a far northwest suburb so that he could stay with a sympathetic aunt who would take him in. He'd spent the last of his money on dinner the night before, so a little extra for food would be appreciated.

I've been around for a long time, something I'm not bragging about. The young man sounded convincing, but, honestly, my gut feeling was that this was probably a scam. The story was too rehearsed, the clothes too clean, and the tears too ready to flow. Even the timing was too perfect; people were starting to enter the church and I had to get everything started. So I gave him twenty dollars and the names of some wonderful support groups, such as the AIDS Pastoral Care Network. I strongly urged him to hook up with them, get on a medication regime, and try to reconcile with his family. That was all we had time for.

A few months later I thought I saw him at a local grocery carrying out a few bags of food. But whoever it was disappeared before I could be sure it was him.

Another month passed and he did reappear, coming to the rectory and asking for me by name. He told me that he had come specifically to thank me for being the only one who had helped him that whole bleak weekend. He had been able to make it out to his aunt's house, and he stayed with her for a week. His efforts to reconcile with his father had failed. But he was able to get himself a room at a friend's apartment. Yes, he had told his friend about his condition. Yes, he was faithfully taking his medication. No, he had not yet found the courage to join a support group. He had just returned from a successful job interview. But he needed ten dollars. And, interestingly, I cannot remember the reason he gave for needing the money.

So do I give it to him a second time? Again, my gut told me that everything sounded too right, too scripted. So this time, even as I found myself handing him the ten-dollar bill, I decided to be direct and honest with him. I shared my doubts and my concerns. I admitted to him that I felt that he could be scamming me and I would never know it. I challenged him by telling him that I hoped his requests were legitimate and that he was using the money for the right reasons and not for drugs or alcohol.

I succeeded in making him cry again, and then again came all the right answers, how he knew that I could feel that way and how truly grateful he was that I was still being so generous. He gave me the name of the friend who had given him the room in which he was staying. He invited me to call his friend to verify everything. He earnestly assured me that when he was on his feet he would pay everything back. He ended by giving me a firm handshake and looking me directly in the eye.

After he left, I kept the card on which he had written down the phone number, but I decided not to call. I'll never know. His problem could be legitimate. Then again, it could be made up, and he could have been counting on my not calling or maybe not caring if at that point I would find out that I had been taken.

I decided that I just did not want to know. I had made my choice. I had tried my best to help someone see that God's love in some small way was available to him. If the story was true, that love would be appreciated. If not, he and his buddies are laughing at me over a beer at a local pub. In either case, someone patiently listened and, however imperfectly, believed him and responded as our faith says we should and as I believe Jesus would have. And maybe that response might eventually hit home and truly touch him in his time of need. Maybe it will come back later and be there for him at a time when he really should remember it. After all, God has been incredibly patient with me. So I can wait on this one. Maybe I'll find out the real story, and maybe I won't. In either case, it's okay. In fact, he's been back and now I don't know. But that's going to be a different story.

homeless christy and a father who holds me

SOMETIMES I JUST LOOK AT MY CALENDAR AND
wonder what I have done to myself. In a particular
day, there may be more to do than I can possibly fit
into my schedule. And if there are unforeseen emer-
gencies to factor in (and there usually are), those days
can be labeled as truly overwhelming. My response is
to become impatient about it all, terrorizing anyone
who gets in my way. This is how it was one particularly hectic day not long ago.

My calendar listed three major time-consuming
activities. The day would begin with a morning
reflection for the teachers in our grammar school.
My topic, ironically, was "Finding the Time to
Make Teaching a Real Ministry." The afternoon
and evening would find me privileged to be at the
Little Sisters of the Poor Nursing Home and Senior
Apartments to celebrate Mass, eat dinner, and give
a Lenten talk on God's unconditional love for us all.

Between these two major commitments was a planning meeting for our clergy convocation. Also, I am scheduled to write the church bulletin and meet with staff members on Mondays, and this was a Monday.

Complicating matters and weighing heavily on me was the outpatient surgery my elderly mother was scheduled to undergo at 11:00 A.M. I knew that I had to be there. So something in my schedule would have to give.

The decision was not difficult. I could send my regrets to those in charge of the meeting on the convocation, hoping to time my arrival at the hospital to coincide with my mother's coming up from the recovery room. I was blessed. I got there just in time to speak with the surgeon who had performed the operation. Things had gone well. He answered all my questions, and I was reassured. Within the half hour, my mother came up from the recovery room and felt better than anyone had expected. However, within the hour they were preparing her to be sent home. I had not anticipated this turn of events. Fortunately, my sister-in-law was there and ready to take her. So with some reluctance I left my mother in my sister-in-law's hands, still somewhat confident that the situation and my schedule were in as good a shape as they could be. But as I waited impatiently for the hospital elevator, I realized that I still could not let go of the tense hold that my too-busy day had on me. I kept looking at my watch.

Distracted, I got on what I expected to be an empty elevator. But I quickly recognized the scent of a person caught up in the snare of poverty and homelessness, someone forced to live on the streets. One of the neighborhood's homeless was on the elevator. To my surprise, it was a woman. Because of how vulnerable women become when they live on the streets, most of them stay out of sight.

Before we had descended even one floor, she was gently tugging on my sleeve, asking, "Are you a priest?" I replied that I was. I glanced at my watch again. "Say a prayer for me, will you?" she asked reverently. As I assured her that I would, I was suddenly overcome by the realization that in the rush and pressure of my busy day, what was now so noticeably missing was prayer. I had no time for it.

I needed to ask her what her name was so that I could respect the person she was. It was "Christy." I then asked Christy if she would in turn pray for me. She seemed genuinely touched by my request. I watched her leave the elevator ahead of me, all of her worldly possessions stuffed into two worn shopping bags. I was incredibly grateful that she had been there to remind me of the importance of prayer and

how, if I patiently found the time for it, it would
help me realize that God is with me and that I need
never feel alone or overwhelmed.

It turned out that I not only survived that day
but also enjoyed it. After everything was over and I
was up in my room, I came across an old black-and-
white photo taken close to half a century ago. It had
fallen out of an album on my bookshelf. In it I am
smiling. I am being lifted up by my arms by my
father. He is swinging me back and forth. I remembered how I felt when Dad did that, and I sensed the
peace and security that I had so often felt in my
father's arms those many years ago. I felt a strange
combination of sadness and comfort—as well as
a little surprise—to be so strongly overcome by that
sensation once again.

At that point, there was no other way for me
to end my day. Prayer was the right response to all
that had happened. So I prayed for the teachers at
the school and for the residents and staff at the Little
Sisters of the Poor. Then I said a very special prayer
for my mother and her health. These were followed
by grateful prayers for Christy. She had made me
slow down. She had reminded me of the necessity of
prayer and had helped me realize that if my prayers
are real and faith filled, time will stand still and I will
know that my God is holding me and protecting me
just as my father did many years ago. I know that the

love that grows from that security will always stay with me and can help me through anything, no matter what. I need only patiently remember to turn to God and place my trust there.

Then I prayed another prayer. It was for my father and it was offered in gratitude for those times he had held me and swung me. It was for those times he had loved me so much that, no matter how busy I was, I could never forget his presence and, because of that, God's presence. I could remember that loving presence in my life from way back then and be aware of it also on this very busy Monday. God will always patiently wait for us to find the time and the way to realize our need to be held and loved and swung around.

flea-bitten

I AM TOLD THAT I'M A NICE GUY, SOMEWHAT
patient, though clearly not to a fault. But there
certainly are times when my Italian temper short-
circuits. And it happens when I least expect it. Not
surprisingly, it usually does more damage to me than
to those caught in its fallout. Those who spend time
around me have learned that my proverbial bark is
bigger than my threatened bite. That word—*bite*—
will be featured prominently in what I am about to
share with you.

I like to think that I am that nice guy. I am, after
all, a cat owner, and all cat owners are nice people. If
you are not a cat owner, you may think differently,
which only proves my point. But I digress.

A broken window in the basement boiler room,
which connects the church and the rectory where
I was living, seemed simple enough to repair when I
reported it to the janitor. But he never got around to

fixing it. With everything else on my mind, I forgot about the window. Then one day, much later, in the laundry room adjacent to the boiler room I found myself face-to-face with a yellow-eyed, very chubby black cat. She took one look at me and ran back into the boiler room, up onto a ledge, and out the broken window. I made a mental note to remind the janitor to fix the window and do it soon.

A week or so later I was back down in the boiler room. Imagine my surprise when I found the black cat, now sleek, standing over a brood of meowing newborn kittens. She was hissing at me and protecting them at the same time. A dead pigeon lay there to feed her and give her the nourishment she needed to pass on to her kittens.

My staff insisted that I leave them all be until the kittens were weaned. We would then offer the kittens up for adoption. We'd let the clearly feral mother go since she would allow no human near her. Then we would seal up that darn window.

For reasons other than the window, the janitor eventually found his way to the boiler room. The mother and her swiftly growing kittens were out foraging for food. Some people had expressed interest in the kittens but had not followed through. And I was still being pressured not to call the anti-cruelty society.

This is how I was rewarded for my niceness (or lack of action). The janitor came up from the basement covered with fleas. His legs quickly grew red with bites. His walking around spread the fleas to the other members of the staff. There could no longer be any inaction on my part. Exterminators were called in, the cats were put outdoors, and the window was fully sealed. We decided that if we could, we'd catch the kittens and take them to an animal shelter. The boiler room was sprayed. Problem solved. But not really. A week later, the poor janitor was reinfested with fleas that had relocated themselves in the nearby laundry room. Unfortunately, before he realized what had happened, the janitor had gone up to my rooms, where Stormy, my fat and sassy, never-a-whisker-outdoors cat, lay sleeping, an unexpected buffet for the arriving fleas. In no time at all she was infested and my rooms were alive with bouncing and jumping little dots of insects.

Stormy, the poor, innocent creature, was transported to a local pet store and dipped. I would have been too but was deemed too large. The cat was isolated until my rooms were thoroughly sprayed. Obviously she was not a happy cat during this process. And this first round of treatment didn't solve the problem. My rooms needed to be sprayed a second time, and my cat needed to be medicated with a prescription just in case.

Even as I write this, I have a crew cleaning out the decades of debris from the basement while armed with cans of bug spray in case they encounter any leftover fleas, filling a Dumpster with garbage and junk, nesting and hiding places for who knows what. As they work on the lower levels of the building, I am cleaning out my closets and nooks and crannies in anticipation of another spraying that will take place in my rooms at the end of the week.

The entire rectory is on "flea alert." I feel like Winston Churchill ready to defend the homeland from invasion. I am confident, despite all the warnings of how hard it will be to clear fleas out of the twenty-eight rooms and basement that comprise our old rectory. But I will do it. I am strangely, calmly patient.

This is a far cry from just a week ago when I was reaching a point of despair. Nothing was working. Sprays, bombs, dippings—the fleas were winning the battle and nothing was working. I desperately wanted them gone. And I wanted them gone immediately.

But if you want something bad enough, you often have to fight for it. This "nice guy" finally got angry enough to silence the critics with one withering look when they started to moan about my putting out some adorable little kittens. I was angry enough to hold onto the janitor's paycheck until the window was properly sealed. And I was angry enough to have everything thrown out of the basement.

On another front I ordered (via overnight express delivery) three ultrasonic contraptions guaranteed to drive fleas out of any house. These contraptions emit a pitch that humans and pets cannot hear. The box said that it would take two weeks, and then all the fleas would be gone. I am willing to wait. I have grown very patient.

Every day I check my cat and then my staff, in that order, for fleas. If the critters return, I will redouble my efforts even if that means closing down the rectory for a day and bombing and spraying every room, closet, and space. This nice guy is determined to win the battle. We'll see.

It seems to me that sometimes our petty selfishness and transgressions must anger and pester God like fleas do cats or a pastor. It is a blessing to know that ours is not a God of thunderbolts who will respond with a scorched-earth policy every time we annoyingly continue our sinful ways. Instead, God remains incredibly patient, working with us, gracing us, knowing that in time, most likely we will respond to all the love and care that is so freely and unconditionally given to us. Ours is a nice God!

Stories of God's Justice

Too often God's justice is experienced as a vengeful, fearful enacting of an eye for an eye and a tooth for a tooth. It may be mirrored in responses we experience from unrelenting teachers, for example. But the pain of loss that can hit us as children when our bicycle has been stolen or as a member of a family that has just lost a daughter and sister to death—

Then Peter went up to him and said, "Lord, how often must I forgive my brother if he wrongs me? As often as seven times?" Jesus answered, "Not seven, I tell you, but seventy-seven times."

~ **MATTHEW 18:21–22**

---

where is God's justice in those times of pain? Is God giving us what we deserve? We must learn that God's justice is never found without God's love also being present. We may experience it as a mother's hand that both corrects and holds us close. To a friend or stranger, we best serve God's justice by sharing God's unconditional love.

summer
dreams

SOMETIMES GOD'S JUSTICE COMES TO US LIKE A
childhood dream, in slow motion, not swift at all,
but weighed down with unexpected love.

First there was the anticipation that began with
the warm winds and longer days of May. Summer vacation would be here, but not soon enough. I would
dream about it over and over again. The last days of
school were painfully long, filled with tedious classroom cleaning chores. It seemed that even the teachers
wanted the school year to end.

Usually I savored every day of vacation. If I
was alone, I'd spend hours playing with plastic soldiers under the big tree in the backyard where the
shade always seemed cooler than it did anywhere
else. I'd pause and dream about being a hero.

When a group of us would gather like a pack
of eager pups, we'd play "war" or "kick the can" or
"fast pitching" until one by one we were called into

our homes for dinner. Rainy days would find me sitting on the unused back staircase behind the pantry, where I was free to daydream about whatever was on my mind. Sometimes I dreamt about being Superman. But usually I dreamt about being able to play with the older kids who hung around with my brothers. They were cool. I was not. So they ignored me. And I was left to dream some more.

But this summer of my twelfth birthday would be special. All the other birthdays in the family came before mine. In my mind, that, along with being the youngest, meant that I never got a special celebration like my brother's, whose Fourth of July birthday always meant a big family celebration tied in with my dad's birthday, which fell in the following week. But come the eighth of August, in the twelfth year of my life, my aunt, who was also my godmother, had promised me a brand-new bicycle. So I couldn't wait for June and July to pass, precious vacation days that they were.

I had walked past the bicycle shop at least a hundred times that summer, the smell of rubber tires and 3-in-1 oil thrilling me every time. I saw the one I wanted. It was a blue Schwinn Spitfire, a middleweight between the heavyweight cruiser bikes and the flimsy lightweight three-speeds. With the blue and white streamers on the handlebars and a speedometer, it would, I was sure, take me wherever my dreams had not yet gone.

Finally the day came. As soon as Carlson's Bike Shop opened on August 8, we were there and my dreams came true. My twenty-four-inch Spitfire meant I could ride with the big boys. I was no longer a little kid. My older brothers would have to take notice of me now. And even if they didn't, I wouldn't care, because on that bike I would become Timmy rescuing Lassie or Spin beating Marty in a horse race and also winning Annette's affections in the process. Dreams would be even more fun when I would be racing in the wind.

Sensibly, Mom bought me a lock and three keys. City living necessitated such precautions even back then. It was second nature to lock up a bike with a thick chain whenever you parked it. I rode my bike from morning until late night every day that first week after my birthday.

It was exactly a week old when I parked it under that tree in our yard and ran into the house to get a drink of water. I didn't lock the bike. I was back in the yard in less than two minutes. But it was gone, and I panicked. Just maybe, one of my brothers had taken it for a ride to tease me. I held on to that hope as long as I could, even promising myself that I would not show how upset I'd become. But, one by one, my brothers came home and not on my bike. I couldn't hold in my grief any longer. I had to tell my mother that it was gone. She asked me how it had happened and then why I hadn't locked it like I had promised to do. She wasn't angry. But the disappointment I heard in her voice over my being too young to responsibly care for such a prized possession added to my pain. She told me I would have to break the news to my aunt.

My reaction was to cry and cry and cry. I could summon up no dreams to sustain me, and worse, I realized that this had become a nightmare from which I could not wake. By the next morning I had a fever. The doctor came and added injury to insult by giving me a painful penicillin shot. But I didn't want to get better. My summer—my life—was ruined. Both might as well end. I was sure that my brothers would tease me over and over again and that I'd never be able to get over the hurt I was feeling.

Three days later, Mom forced me to get out of my bed. She ordered me to go outside and play. My brothers were standing in the yard when I walked outside. I immediately got a sinking feeling in my stomach. They ordered me to come with them. My feet were like lead. I promised myself that I would not cry no matter what they did to me.

We went down the back stairs into the cellar where we kept our bikes. No, the Spitfire wasn't there. I saw their three bikes leaning lazily on their kickstands, and I felt how unfair life had become. Then I noticed it. They had taken the old eighteen-inch kiddie bike that we had all learned to ride on, stripped off its dented fenders, painted it jet black, bought some ebony handle grips and silver streamers, and polished the chrome spokes. By reversing the handlebar and installing a sleek new black racing seat raised as high as it could go, my brothers had created for me a bicycle equivalent of a hot rod.

We all knew that it couldn't replace the Spitfire. It didn't. But at least it was something. And I knew that riding it would allow me to dream of finding my precious bike somewhere and scaring off the thieves; they would see me on this lean, mean, stripped-down, no-nonsense tough guy's bike and run off in fear.

I started to cry, not at what I had lost but at what I had found: brothers who loved me enough to want me to keep dreaming. I couldn't help it. They saw my tears and laughed, walking away thinking I was still a little squirt who cried. But that was okay with me. God's justice had come to me through my brothers' love for me. They wouldn't understand—at least not then—how much they had helped me grow up during that dream-filled, grace-filled summer of my twelfth year.

hardheaded

MATH WAS NEVER ONE OF MY STRONG ACADEMIC
subjects. From algebra (the numbers and letters made
my head spin) to geometry (points and lines leading
nowhere) to trigonometry (I still don't know what
that is all about), my grades in high school got pro-
gressively lower each year. Thank God there was no
senior year of math or I might still be there trying
to graduate. I am one of the few people I know who
earned a college degree and an advanced degree
without having to take any higher education mathematics classes. Call me lucky.

I certainly would not have used that phrase
back in my junior year of high school as I struggled
through the maze of confusion that was to my classmates trigonometry but was to me just a mystery. My
teacher was a portly priest who taught from a seated
position only and behind an imposing desk. By the
bad luck of the alphabet, I ended up in the first seat

of the middle row right in front of him. This meant that I not only had to stay awake but I also seemed to get called on an inordinate number of times. And he used so much Old Spice cologne that very often on warm days I would feel sick. To this day, anyone wearing that scent enters into an adversarial relationship with me through absolutely no fault of his own.

In a vain, foolhardy, but valiant attempt to move the teacher off of his usual seat and away from me, I confess to having placed a thumbtack on his chair. I was dumbstruck when he sat down and nothing happened! Did he swipe it away secretly? Or was he stoically bearing the pain so as not to give the perpetrator any satisfaction? Neither. When I discretely checked after class, I found that he had by his very girth bent the sharp point of the tack flat. I gave up.

One Sunday, facing a major test the next morning, I decided somewhat halfheartedly to study. I hoped that whatever I might be able to learn would stay with me at least until after the exam the next morning. But fate got in the way. Sunday morning the family piled into the Chrysler, and Dad, letting my brother Tony drive, headed us in the vague direction of St. Joseph College in Indiana to visit my brother Felix, who had magically Americanized himself into Phil in the midst of the cornfields of the Hoosier state.

The trip there was uneventful. The visit was actually boring. My brother Phil was such a clean-cut collegian that there was nothing in his dorm room of interest to a curious younger brother. The ride home would prove to be a different story. Not five minutes away from the campus, Tony, who was used to straight city streets, took a country hairpin curve a little too quickly and hit an oncoming car head-on.

Mom and Dad were in the backseat. Mom broke a rib and Dad his nose. My brother's girlfriend was next to him, leaving me in the front passenger-side seat, often labeled ominously the "death" seat. I put my head through the windshield. Tony's girl-friend and future wife, whom he had gallantly shielded, was okay, as was he. I remember her very kindly saying to me, "Please don't bleed."

"I'm trying not to," I responded.

The rest of the day was a blur. Nobody wanted to go to a hospital in the small town. So Mom and Dad got a lift home to Chicago from other visiting parents. Phil arrived and made my brother Tony drive the rest of us back to campus. With my splitting headache, I didn't think that was such a good idea since he was the one who had gotten us into the accident. But it did prove to restore his shaken confidence.

We took a bus back to Chicago, where I was sent to a hospital for some precautionary X-rays of my head. Not surprisingly, my head proved to be harder than the glass it had shattered. With no fracture or concussion I was supposed to take aspirin and sleep the headache off on Monday, which I did.

So on Tuesday I walked into math class wearing a bandage and a victorious smile. I had missed the test and I had a doctor's note! The teacher read the note and without a word handed me a copy of the test. I protested, saying that I wasn't able to study Sunday evening because of the headache or on Monday either. "Read the note again," I begged him. His smile was even more sickening than his Old Spice. "Why didn't you study on Saturday night?" he asked.

"I wasn't planning to be in an accident on Sunday." I'm sure this desperate response was taken as insolence.

"Well," he said, "never put off to tomorrow what you could have done today." He sent me next door to another class to take the test in the back of the room. The kindly Latin teacher, seeing my distress, asked if I was feeling alright. I just grunted and sat down to most certainly flunk a major test.

For a while I just stared at the questions blankly and fought off my stubbornness and hardheadedness. I wanted to either just put anything down or hand it in blank. Before I knew it the bell had rung and somehow I had a real answer for each of the questions, something unusual for me. I brought the test to my teacher and gave it to him without a word.

The next day he handed it back to me without a word as well. I had a grade I wasn't expecting, an 85 percent, which was a low B, my best grade ever in that class. A classmate informed me that with the curve my grade averaged out to an A minus.

I found out later that my teacher made a point of checking with the Latin teacher to make sure I could not have cheated. The Latin teacher let him know that no one cheated under his supervision and then added that I had looked too sick to have even been given the test. Chalk one up for the good guys!

The test score carried me through the course well enough to earn a low C as my final grade. And I was as happy with it as I would have been with any A. In my mind, it was all divine intervention. It wasn't luck or the fact that my anger or my headache or both so distracted me from my fear of failure that what I did know came out. No. It was, pure and simple, God's justice. What I deserved from that intolerant and tyrannical teacher was a break. I didn't get it. So God stepped in and gave me what I deserved and maybe even a little more.

striking
out

I FELT, ON THAT PARTICULAR SUNDAY, THAT I
was being relevant, preaching about baseball. Earlier
in the week, in their fight to get into the playoffs, the
Chicago Cubs had found a new and amazingly heart-
breaking way to lose a crucial game. The opposing
team had come up to bat. It was their last chance, the
bottom of the ninth inning. The bases were loaded,
and they needed all three of those runners to score
in order to win. There were two outs on the team
and two strikes on the batter. He hit a lazy fly ball
to the Cubs' left fielder, who had just come into the
game for defensive purposes. He barely needed to
move a step. He calmly put his sunglasses down,
confidently pounded his fist into his glove, and waited for the ball to land securely in his mitt. But to
his surprise and to that of every spectator, the ball
dropped to the ground. All three runners scored,
and in that brief moment the Cubs lost the game.

Once again, long-suffering Cubs fans had their hearts broken in disbelief. It was all people talked about for a week.

In my mind I would masterfully tie in what happened to the Cubs with the Gospel of the parable of Lazarus, Abraham, and the rich man who would get the justice he deserved. And that is how on a warm Sunday morning I found myself actually preaching that life is like a baseball game and that since we will never know when it is the last play of the final inning we need to remember that God will deal with us justly.

I knew that I was stretching it a bit, but it was fitting together even better than I had hoped. Then, in the middle of it, a poorly dressed, disheveled man walked into the church. He started walking up the middle aisle and genuflected no more than five feet from where I was preaching. It was a distraction to a number of people in the congregation.

But being the old pro that I am, I continued on as best I could, even as I focused on him. Having been preaching for over a quarter of a century, I have learned that it is easy enough to be saying the words of your sermon to the congregation even as you find yourself thinking about something entirely different.

So as I continued on, I was thinking that this was a con artist trying to impress all of us with his exaggerated piety. I figured that after Mass he would give me some sad story and hit me up for ten or twenty dollars—in front of parishioners with whom he'd hope I would want to save face. *Well,* I thought, *he's not getting anything from me at all.* Finally, having been distracted so much, I put a rather abrupt ending to the homily.

The man continued to distract the congregation. And through the Prayer of the Faithful I found myself thinking that these guys will do anything for money. During the recitation of the Creed I hoped he wouldn't also hit up the parishioners. During the presentation of gifts, as the ushers were taking up the collection, I wished that they were more aggressive in keeping these people out of the church. I continued to wonder if my point about being ready for the end of our lives by doing well today was communicated and if people saw the analogy I tried to make with the last out of a baseball game. I knew that if this guy hadn't walked up the aisle, I could have spelled it out better.

These thoughts were in my mind even as I was preparing for the consecration of the bread and wine. Then, without warning, something disturbing passed through my mind, from where I do not know. *You idiot. Can't you see that this man who came into church poorly dressed and is now kneeling directly in front of you at this sacred moment—he is your Lazarus?* As I consecrated the bread I realized that I was no better than the rich man who begrudged Lazarus the scraps that the man fed to his dogs. Here I was, self-righteously preaching to others about taking the opportunity to reach out to those in need before it was too late, while I was so ready to write off this man because of his appearance and so smugly sure that I knew exactly what his agenda was.

I found myself sitting a little longer in my postcommunion meditation. I pictured myself, the final inning over—the entire game of my life over—and I had just committed this major error. There I was, asking for a little water for my parched lips, for a little comfort. And looking up to heaven I saw this man, who was now lost in quiet prayer in the pew, sitting radiantly in the lap of Abraham and telling me kindly that there was no way he could help me. And if that weren't enough, then I started seeing other Lazaruses I had prejudged, ignored, and even mistreated. Before I stood up for the final blessing, I knew I would have to talk to this man after Mass.

But as is sometimes the case, lots of people came up to me that day. Ironically, some wanted to tell me how much they liked my sermon. Others simply wanted to talk about the Cubs' chances. Some had questions about Pre-Cana or Baptismal Preparation class. And then there were babies to be blessed and assurances to be made to others that prayers would be offered for their needs. Someone stopped me and asked about a particular wedding date. I was so busy that I forgot about the man who had become my Lazarus. I never saw him leave.

When the crowds cleared and I finally went back into the church, it was pretty much empty. The man was nowhere to be seen. I began to doubt that anyone else in the congregation had even noticed him, at least not like I had. He was gone, but I couldn't forget him.

I preached the same homily one more time at a later Mass. But my heart wasn't in it. Listening to myself, I felt shallow and dishonest. My delivery was flat and lacked energy. I was sorry that I had not been able to practice what I'd been preaching.

In fact, the real sermon that I should have preached that second time around are these very reflections, which I wrote down later in the day. I put them on paper so that I could admit that I had struck out when I should have hit a home run. At least I was fortunate that this day was not the last inning of my game. I don't deserve them, but God has given me additional innings to become more open and understanding of future Lazaruses who come into my life.

We should be grateful that God doesn't always give us what we deserve. God's justice is always tempered by God's love and forgiveness—and another inning.

one saint's day

I READ SOMEWHERE THAT THE BISHOPS OF THE United States have more than once brought up for discussion among themselves the issue of holy days of obligation: how many we should have and what feasts should be celebrated. As of this writing, they have decided not to make any changes. Some cynics might suggest that perhaps there is some concern among the bishops that if the numbers were lessened, fewer envelopes would find their way into the collection basket. I will choose not to touch that charged issue with a ten-foot pole, or a crosier for that matter. Bishops have their reasons.

However, I would like to stand up for one of those days that we currently celebrate, the one referred to as All Saints' Day. Many know it as the day after Halloween. But my reasons go well beyond the great children's celebration that occurs on its eve. My only suggestion would be to change its name to "One Saint's Day."

Why? I think that by trying to celebrate all of these good and deserving people collectively, we are not able to properly single out and honor that one saintly person now deceased who has had such an especially profound impact on us and our lives. If we are blessed with more than one such person, we could very easily honor them individually on this date in successive years. This could make November 1 an important and truly holy day for us because we would honor these special ones who have done so much for us from heaven. It is only just and fitting that we owe them this day.

I would honor my sister, who died at the young age of seven, just ten months before I was born. I am told that she was a bright and gifted child often sent by her teachers up to the eighth-grade class to show off her reading skills. She also played the piano well enough to be featured in school recitals. Her pictures reveal a beautiful child with dark, curly hair, piercing eyes, and a smile that would melt the hardest of hearts.

One fateful day she came home from school and announced that she had decided to become a nun when she grew up. My mother was on her knees scrubbing the bathroom at the time and remembers that she stopped and prayed that God would not take her only daughter from her like that. That prayer would haunt my mom for the rest of her life. She would always feel that God punished her by taking her daughter from her because she wasn't willing to give her up to the service of God. Nothing would ever change Mom's mind or keep her from feeling that incredible pain.

In the forties, if a child complained of a stiff neck and developed a high fever, a parent's worst fear would be hearing the dreaded word *polio*. My sister was rushed to the county hospital and placed immediately into an infectious-disease ward with other suffering children. My parents could only watch from a distance, separated from her by a glass partition. She would not live beyond the weekend. The only consolation was that she was able to receive her First Holy Communion on her deathbed.

And so they chose to bury her in her white communion dress, the one she would never be able to wear with her classmates. Even at the funeral home, a glass wall kept my parents separated from her, their oldest child, their only daughter. The undertaker, seeing my mother distraught to the point of collapse, took a metal Sacred Heart of Jesus pendant that was hanging on the casket and gave it to her. In doing so, he no doubt broke some health laws, but he must have known that she desperately needed something to hold on to. It hangs in my room today.

My father, in his grief, never spoke his daughter's name until he was on his deathbed forty years later, when he called out for her gently, reached out his arms as though she was coming to him, and then took a last breath with a peaceful smile on his face. My mother's grief over my sister's death turned my mother's hair so completely white that when I was born ten months later, strangers thought that she was my grandmother.

But somehow that grief did not lead to bitterness, which could have happened if my mother had held onto my sister's death as an injustice from a punishing God. Instead, over the years, my mother has shared with her children the profound closeness she has retained with her daughter.

So, like my brothers, I have a framed picture of my sister in my room. My parent's first grandchild was named for her: Annamaria. I pray to my sister and talk to her as I would to an older, living sister. Like every family, ours has had its share of illness, problems, and heartbreaks. And we have also had our share of blessings, miracles, and graced moments. Through everything, we have always remained incredibly close. I have been truly blessed to baptize my brothers' children and later marry them and now even baptize their children.

Take any of us aside and ask us why our lives have been as good as they have been, why we all feel blessed well beyond anything that we deserve, and eventually we will each in our own way talk to you about Annamaria, our precious sister, the young child who had wanted to serve God and who has been watching out for us from her place in heaven.

Where can we find justice in the death of such an innocent one? To simply say that God's ways are not ours is not too facile an answer. It is the reality. We cannot ask, "What if she had lived?" because she did not. But God did not love her or my mother or us any less. Annamaria's life and death have taught us never to ask "Why?" of God. Rather we have come to realize that God's love is given to us in very mysterious and awesome ways.

She continues to intercede for us. Isn't that what saints are supposed to do? And that is why she is the one I want to—and will—celebrate on the Feast of All Saints' Day, rather, the Feast of One Saint's Day. I will celebrate and honor one beautiful little girl who died for reasons we will never know and who yet has remained such an important part of our family now and for generations to come.

Happy feast day, Annamaria. And thank you for all you do for your family.

visiting the suburbs

THERE IS SOME IRONY IN THE FACT THAT SO
many peasants from the small towns and farms of
southern Italy ended up coming to these United
States and settling in big urban areas like Chicago.
For reasons I will never know, our family didn't
settle in a traditional Italian neighborhood. So for
many years the only Italians I knew were family
or people who worked in the family grocery store.
My world consisted of the streets and alleys and
gangways of the city. Like many Italians who lived
in the city, my grandfather was able to turn a dark
corner of soil along the side of the house into a
garden filled with tomatoes, cucumbers, peppers, and
herbs of all sorts. But eventually, some of these city
dwellers would buy themselves a home in the suburbs, where there were wide streets, identical little
houses, and not a tree's worth of shade to be found.
They would proudly extend to us poor city folk an

invitation to visit them there, and off we would go on a Sunday adventure.

One distant set of relatives invited us to their new home for an old-fashioned all-American picnic. It was a good idea but one that these transplanted Italians did not quite grasp. So there we were, in a backyard with no tree or shade, sitting in the sun, the thermometer breaking ninety, on metal chairs, resting our hands on a hot aluminum table. Imagine our surprise when the hostess began the meal by serving piping hot minestrone soup followed by bowls and bowls of steaming pasta. At my age I did not know what heat stroke was, but I knew I was on the verge of being struck down by it.

On still another Sunday, the family accepted an invitation from other relatives and off we drove, further than anticipated, to a far distant suburb, a "planned community," my father called it with a quizzical tone to his voice. It was an awesome sight: house after identical house, all lined up on streets that curved and arched and dead-ended with no rhyme or reason. Dad did a lot of muttering and backtracking, and we arrived a good hour late.

After dinner the adults slipped as usual into a spirited conversation. Unfortunately it wasn't in English. No one offered to turn on the television. We children were supposed to sit still and politely pretend that this was a fun way to spend the afternoon.

Finally, crashing boredom got the better of me. After feigning a trip to the bathroom, I wandered through the house and eventually ended up in the attached garage. To my surprise, its door had been left open, something I never saw in the city. And there before my eyes was a shiny new bicycle, just waiting for me to take it for a ride. No ten-year-old could resist such a temptation. And I didn't.

The streets were wide. There were no stop-lights, no trucks, no buses, hardly any cars, and almost nobody walking since there were no sidewalks either. I rode like the Lone Ranger going to rescue Tonto, like Hopalong Cassidy trying to catch a fleeing villain. I rode up one street and down another. The next thing I knew, the sun had already begun to set, and I needed to head back as quickly as I could.

But where was back? After riding aimlessly for a few blocks, I realized that I was completely lost. I didn't know what the house looked like, except that it looked exactly like every other house around me. I did know that the street it was on had a girl's name. But the developer of that subdivision must have had lots of daughters or girlfriends; every street was a girl's name. I rode up Donna Lane, crossed Bonnie Drive, passed Lisa Street and Anna Avenue, stopped in Kristen Circle, turned down Laura Boulevard, and wondered what a Gina Cul-de-sac was.

Almost instantly, confusion turned to fear, fear of the enclosing darkness, of being lost, and worse yet, of being found. Dad always liked to be on the road before it was dark. I even wondered if the family might have left without me. I pedaled up and down street after street, not sure if I was covering the same territory. But I was too afraid to stop and could see no one to ask. So I kept on pedaling.

Finally, after rounding a corner, I saw a group of twenty or so people walking down the middle of the wide street. Some were shining flashlights in the bushes of the houses, in the air, and up the street. It was all too reminiscent of the mob scene in *Frankenstein*. The lights caused me to freeze. I adjusted my eyes and realized that my little five-foot mother was leading the search party.

I jumped from the bicycle and ran to her as fast as my weary, rubbery legs would carry me. I was so happy to see her that I forgot just for a moment why everyone was out there looking for me. It came jolting back to my senses when Mom's left hook (thank God she wasn't holding the flashlight in that hand) landed on the backside of my head. In quick succession came the questions: Where were you? Are you okay? Don't you know (a) how late it is? (b) how worried we were? (c) how mad your father back at the house is? (d) what you did wrong? There were more. I forget them now.

The crowd turned and headed back to the house. Wouldn't you know it, it was fifty feet away. Mom and I trailed the group. I was expecting a few more "reminders" from her left hand. Instead she placed her hand in mine and squeezed it warmly. Without her saying a word, I knew that she loved me and had been worried and was now happy that I was okay. I realized that her original blow was for everyone to see that I got what I deserved and so that she could tell Dad that she had sufficiently handled it.

"I love you Mom," I said, and she squeezed my hand again.

Sometimes we confuse God's justice with our own feelings of guilt, and we forget that God's love is always the overriding response to our actions. No matter what happens, God's love and forgiveness go beyond what we feel we may deserve if we've been lost for a while.

Stories of God's Absence

In moments of loss, anxiety, sorrow, or loneliness, when God seems terrifyingly absent, two things can happen. God may somehow be there in our pain, hoping that we will encounter the love that is the unmistakable sign of that presence. Or in the abject, total emptiness that we experience, we might be graced to grow more acutely aware of those times in

> When the sixth hour came there
> was darkness over the whole land
> until the ninth hour. And at the
> ninth hour Jesus cried out in
> a loud voice, "Eloi, Eloi, lama
> sabachthani?" which means,
> "My God, my God, why have
> you deserted me?"
>
> ~ MARK 15:33–34

---

the past when God has been with us. In the darkness
of a forest or the darkness of an angry death, when
cruelty is inflicted on us or when our cruelty is inflicted
on strangers, and even in the fatalism communicated
by shrugged shoulders—we owe it to ourselves to
override that sense of God's absence with the belief
that we will find God somewhere, somehow.

shrugging shoulders

EVERY SUNDAY, THE TWO OF THEM CAME TO
church together, clearly dressed for the occasion.
As he held the heavy church door open for her, I
would inevitably catch a whiff of the strong cigars
he enjoyed while sitting on the front stoop of their
house, just a block down from the church. He would
give me a courtly "tip of the hat," and then they
would proceed to the same pew they had knelt and
sat in side by side for decades.

Once, I was surprised by the quick flare of his
temper. It happened when the route they normally
took to church had been blocked off for our summer
festival. I assured him that it would be perfectly
acceptable for him and his wife to walk through the
closed-off area. He quickly calmed down.

When word came to me early one morning
of his wife's sudden death, I was genuinely saddened.
I felt bad for him. I wondered how he would cope

with being alone and losing his life's partner. At her wake, he seemed dazed, shrugging his shoulders in resignation to all those who came to offer their sympathies. He looked a little tattered around the edges and older by far than he had the week before. I wondered if she was the one who laid out his clothes and gave him a final inspection before they went out the door. Probably.

At the funeral his eyes were red and tear filled. He looked confused and lost. He seemed, despite his family sitting all around him, as if he was alone in the pew. At the cemetery, when I began to bless the coffin with holy water, the head of the sprinkler I was using inexplicably flew off, bouncing on the metal of the casket and careening past his ear. The room fell silent as, stunned, everyone looked at him, waiting for his temper to flare. Instead he just shrugged his shoulders as if to ask, "What else could happen?" And before I could stammer out an apology, he just smiled at me affectionately and said he knew that I would do something to make everyone laugh. Then he proudly announced that he had obviously picked out the best coffin in which to place his wife, the proof being that the heavy sprinkler head had not even scratched the finish.

Since then he would occasionally stop by the rectory. It gave him something to do. His shirts were wrinkled and stained. More often than not, he was unshaven. The smell of his cigars always lingered. He would come by frequently to have Mass celebrated in his wife's memory. One time he stopped by and was his old self again. He was very angry with me because his year-end financial statement from the parish was wrong. And he let me know in no uncertain terms that if we did not want his money, he would find somewhere else to worship. I just talked with him until his anger subsided. He gave me a soft shrug, apologized, and simply remarked on how lonely he was.

Another time he came by to tell me about the trip he was planning back to Italy. He was very animated and the most excited I had seen him in a long time. A few weeks later, when I asked him how his plans were going, he told me with a shrug that they had fallen through due to another illness and subsequent death in his family. Loss and that debilitating sense of absence were becoming an ongoing part of his life.

He had also taken to coming to early morning Mass daily for solace, but also, he told me, because he was awake, unable to sleep much at night. And it gave him something to do and someplace to go.

Many times as I would be rushing to my car in the garage or over to church or across the street to the school and hall, I would see him slowly walking down the block. A few times I would catch up to him and we would sit and talk, mostly about nothing. After a while he would get up and look around with a shrug and walk away with no particular destination in mind. It seemed that he was searching for something that he could not accept was no longer there.

He fell and had to have his arm in a sling. When I asked him how he was doing, the embers of his temper flared briefly. It was a dumb question. Could I possibly realize how hard it was for him to do everything for himself? I realized that he was not just talking about his disabled arm. He was barely making it through his days with help from painkillers and antidepressants. Visits from grandchildren seemed to be a little more helpful. But mostly he had continuing loneliness and loss and the daily painful absence of his wife to cope with.

He began to repeat the same thing to me whenever we would talk. He admitted being angry. He felt that he was the one who was supposed to die first. I seldom knew what to say in response. In my frustration, I finally asked him if, had it happened like he expected it would, would he really want his wife to be sitting here feeling the way he was feeling now, so alone and sad? His response was to stand up slowly and shrug his shoulders silently, just as he did at the cemetery and the same way he always did. Once again accidentally I had brought everything, like a careening hunk of metal bouncing off a coffin, to the point of absurdity, leaving both of us speechless. And so as he walked away, I could only get up and silently shrug back.

He has recently moved away, begrudgingly, to be close to his children and grandchildren. Actually, they wanted to be closer to him. I do miss him. I feel his absence, but nowhere near as much as I am certain he still misses his wife and also the God who became absent to him when she died. I hope that he will someday find them both.

yes, miss daley

SHE WAS ONE OF ONLY TWO LAY TEACHERS IN
the entire school. Back then there were more than
enough Sisters of Mercy to go around. But, unfortunately, for some reason, Miss Daley was in our school.
She had always been there. And in our young minds,
she would always be there in the same room, year
after year, teaching sixth grade.

Like the nuns but without the benefit of
a religious habit, she was obviously old, but we
couldn't tell how old. Her gray hair resembled
a large dandelion puff floating on the air through
the summer breezes. And when she ran her hands
through it in exasperation—which was often—
screaming at the class, "I cannot hear you!" more
than a few of those hairs would fly off quite dramatically. I was sure that some day, given her penchant
for screaming, she would have no hair left to run
her hands through.

Each year a new group of sixth graders would come to her room like new recruits. Within two weeks she would have the entire class responding as one to whatever her questions were with a hearty "Yes, Miss Daley!" or "No, Miss Daley!" And if the volume of the group was not to her satisfaction, she would in turn respond to us with her "I cannot hear you!" If our response still was not loud enough, she'd add the command "Get up!" and we'd jump out of our seats, screaming our response as loudly as we could.

Consequently, she and we as a class were altogether too loud. It used to give me a headache. I wondered if perhaps she was hard of hearing. In any case, when guests came to our classroom, we would unintentionally scare the wits out of them. Imagine the poor young college girl brought in to teach us art once a week saying in her soft voice, "Will you please take out your Crayolas" and having us mechanically shout into her face, "Yes, Miss Daley!" Taken aback, she'd mutter, "I'm Miss Green. Call me Miss Green." To which we'd all, like automatons, shout, "Yes, Miss Daley!" We'd look over at Miss Daley and she'd be smiling contently, her lips more noticeably pursed because of the streak of red lipstick she would use only when a guest was coming to the room.

Miss Daley hated creativity of any sort. We were to color only between the lines and write poetry in perfect iambic pentameter using the script of the Palmer Method without any hint of variation. Learning equaled memorization, and vice versa. Math tables existed to be recited over and over again, as were responses to the Baltimore Catechism. And if we faltered, we'd be accused of the most horrendous crime—daydreaming—and we'd be banished to "Sleepy Hollow," which was the name she gave to the first two rows of desks, the ones closest to the bulletin boards and to her wrath.

Sitting in a boy-girl-boy-girl configuration, the students in those two rows contained the most frightened students you would ever see. They often looked like deer trapped and stunned by oncoming, speeding headlights. Being in Sleepy Hollow meant that Miss Daley gave them what she called "special treatment" by calling on them even if they didn't raise their hands. And God protect them if they did not answer correctly. It was an even worse crime if you froze and were not able to say anything at all. I remember when that happened to David, whom Miss Daley proceeded to grab and throw against the blackboard. When the slate cracked and fell to the floor, she hit him on the head with her yardstick. How dare he damage her room.

Sadly, most of the occupants of Sleepy Hollow were children of color, some newly arrived from other countries, whose only problem was being unable to respond quickly enough in English. Miss Daley would brand them daydreamers and, mocking their accents, toss them into Sleepy Hollow. One student was so intimidated that he was reduced to a stammer every time he tried to respond. For that she gave Harry the title of "Mayor of Sleepy Hollow."

Quite honestly, I think that the rest of us were relieved that, unjust as it was, most of our teacher's wrath was directed away from us and to those unfortunate ones in Sleepy Hollow. One day when my mind wandered to thoughts of summer vacation and fishing and riding my bike, Miss Daley called me to the front of the room and asked me what was so funny. My honest answer was "Nothing, Miss Daley." Since she had seen me smiling, she took my answer as a lie. She asked me again what I was doing. I didn't know what else to say but the truth. So I blurted out, "Daydreaming." She thought I was mocking her. She grabbed her purse, which looked and weighed like a bowling bag, and hit me over the head with it. I saw stars. Thank God it was the end of the school day. Was that the school bell or just ringing in my ears? She said she would take care of me tomorrow.

When I got home, I asked my mom for an aspirin. She wanted to know why. I told her what had happened, figuring that since I was already in trouble with Miss Daley, Mom would find out about it after I landed in Sleepy Hollow the next day. Mom did look displeased at me for not paying attention, but she seemed genuinely upset when I told her about the purse, my head, the stars, and the bells.

The next day I was surprised that I wasn't moved to Sleepy Hollow as I had expected. Instead, Miss Daley was solicitous to me all day long. I finally realized that I was more than lucky: Mom must have called the principal. But I also knew that Mom wouldn't always be there to save me. So during my sixth-grade year I never again dared to daydream about fishing or riding my bike or anything else for that matter.

And while my "Yes, Miss Daley!" was the loudest in the classroom, I had lost something precious. It would take me years to realize that I needed it and even longer to restore it.

Children need to daydream. Without those dreams, God is absent in their little hearts. Because for children it is precisely in those dreams where God is most present.

sandy

IN MY PERSONAL BIBLE IS A YELLOWING
three-by-five card with this simple quotation centered on it:

> *We need to have PEOPLE
> who mean something to us,
> people to whom we can turn
> knowing that being with them
> is coming HOME.*

It then says, "In memory of . . ." and gives
Sandy's name with the date of her birth and the date
of her death twenty-eight years later.

I have attended countless numbers of wakes
and celebrated too many funerals in my years of
ministry. Unlike some priests, I do not collect
remembrance cards except for a special few. Sandy's
has no picture on it of a saint or a peaceful pastoral
scene. It has no cross, no sunrise. She wasn't a rela-
tive or even a friend. At best, she was a friend of a

friend of mine. I had gotten to know her just briefly before her death. So I am not too sure why I keep her card in my Bible. Perhaps it is because of how she died and the impact her death had on me. I can't and don't want to forget it, while at the same time I wish that I could.

I was introduced to Sandy only a year or so before her death. Her friends had hoped that her getting to know me both as a priest and as someone her own age might get her to open up and help her deal with her issues.

When I first met Sandy, the ravages of her illness had not yet taken their toll on her, at least not on her body. But clearly her spirit was diseased. She was incredibly angry. And her anger was directed to just about everyone. Consequently, her circle had shrunk to just two loyal friends. She was even angry with strangers on the street and workers in the stores, treating them with contempt and leaving them puzzled as to why they had elicited such a response from her. Most of all, she was angry with herself. And she showed that anger in her appearance. I don't think I ever saw her wearing anything but tattered jeans and a rumpled sweatshirt. She was always unkempt, never combing her hair or using any makeup.

But most of all, Sandy was angry with God. Hers was an anger so deep and so hard that it would take away your ability to respond to her and make you impotently speechless. There was just nothing you could say to her when she spat out her story to you. And, indeed, it was a pain-filled story.

Sandy's mother had been diagnosed with cancer. It was, as it all too often can be, a cruel disease that led up to a most painful death. Sandy, as her caretaker, could not help but be caught up in that pain. It was no wonder then that when Sandy herself was diagnosed with that very same cancer shortly after her mother died, her feelings would swing from paralyzing fear to red-hot anger. She clearly knew the path down which the disease would ultimately lead her. It was not fair, and in her mind she came to believe that God was mocking her.

She was neither easy to talk to nor fun to be around. Some people even whispered that her very attitude made her condition worse and spread the deadly disease's poison even more quickly through her body.

I really wasn't able to be much help to her. I'm not sure that anyone could have been at that point in her life. Finally, I came home late one night and found a series of frantic phone messages from her friends calling from the hospital. The end was coming, and they wanted me there as soon as possible.

When I rushed into the hospital room, I was frankly surprised that Sandy was still conscious and remarkably alert. But I was not at all surprised that she had been giving her friends a hard time. In fact, as I walked in, she was flashing an obscene gesture at them, the tubes in her throat and nose making it too difficult to talk. They looked at me in desperation, hoping that I would be able to do something. Amazingly, when Sandy saw me, the gesture transformed into an open hand, which she allowed me to take into mine. I sat down next to her and prepared myself for a long night. And it was.

At first I tried to make small talk. She looked away and was not interested at all. When I then suggested that we pray, she looked me right in the eyes and nearly broke the bones in my hand with her furious grip. Finally, I told her that I would pray. She nearly yanked my arm out of its socket. I gave up. I just sat there quietly, still holding her hand. This she assented to with a begrudging nod of her head.

There were very few interruptions during the night. When hospital workers realize that they can no longer heal, they seem to unintentionally separate themselves from the patient. I guess this is only normal. So I sat there with Sandy's hand in mine. I was praying that somehow in her few remaining moments she would let go of all her anger and die in peace. Part of me truly believed that she would come around, that no one would choose to die so angry and fight God until the end.

But Sandy did. Even as she drifted into unconsciousness, I could still feel and sense the struggle that was going on inside of her.

When her last breath came, it was with the same desperation with which all the previous ones had come. No peaceful countenance came over her troubled face, nor any hint of resolution. Her hand, despite the weakness that gradually progressed through the rest of her body, tightened its grip on mine. When Sandy was finally pronounced dead, I needed to use my free hand to pry open her fingers from around my hand, which was starting to feel numb. Even in death, Sandy refused to let go.

Before I left, I took one final look at her and felt a coldness envelop me. I tried to find consolation in the fact that her struggle was finally over and that she could now be embraced by a loving God whose presence had always been with her even though she could not feel or sense or believe it. She was finally home.

But all I felt was a hollowness that filled the air and made it hard for me to catch my breath. It was an emptiness that frightened me. Where was God? I did not look back again as I left the hospital room. I needed to look forward at the sun that was just starting to rise over the city. It was morning and I was so glad to be alive.

lost in
muir woods

DRIVING DOWN THE COASTAL HIGHWAY IN
California at different times in my life, I have come
to experience the presence of God in quite distinct
ways. The first unforgettable opportunity occurred
when I was riding in the back of a twenty-five-foot
Winnebego motor home driven by a classmate
after a group of us had spent the warm afternoon
tasting wine in Sonoma Valley. No one had bothered
to inform us that real wine tasters discretely spat
out their wine. We were quite content to chug our
way through merlots and chardonnays with wild
abandon.

I knew that I was in no shape to drive. But I
was not blessed with falling asleep, as were two other
classmates. So I stared with terror at how close the
rear end of this large camper was coming to the edge
of the highway and the hundred-foot drop just inches
away from the tires. "My God! My God!" was all I

could bring myself to say. It was part curse, part petition, and mostly contrition.

The second occurrence was a few years later and a little further south, when I was driving the premium symbol of southern California, a little two-seater convertible rented just for this occasion. The warmth of the sun was on my head, the wind was in my face, and I was watching small clouds of fog work their way inland over the roadway. I had brought my camera with me, but I knew that no picture would do that vision justice. So I finally had to stop driving and just admire the heavenly beauty of it all. I wanted to sear the meaning of it into my memory and my heart. God was there as sure as I was.

A third trip down the same road became a special moment in time when, as I gazed out at the sand, the surf, and the small rock formation in the water, I saw all at once a school of dolphins dancing in the water and a herd of seals (or is it a flock or simply a bunch?) sunning themselves on a craggy, tiny island. So much beauty of God's creation right in my line of vision! It was a sacred moment that passed all too quickly. Once again, I knew that I had been in the presence of the Sacred.

So when I took a fourth trip some time later, it was with a great deal of anticipation. This time I was going with a good friend far enough south to experience the giant redwoods of Muir Woods. Turning from the highway into the forest, the first feeling I noticed was that it simultaneously grew cooler and quieter. It reminded me of walking into a cathedral from a busy city street. I found myself speaking in hushed and reverent tones. This was going to be a very special time.

We parked the car and got ready to walk. A sign indicated that the park closed promptly at dusk. But the sun still dappled through the branches so incredibly high above us. We had plenty of time. My other senses soon took notice of the incredibly strong pine scent in the air and the remarkably soft pine needles that made it feel like we were walking on an ultrathick carpet.

Where to go? There were many helpful signs, which was fortunate because no other folks were around us. The eight-mile walk seemed a bit too much of a good thing. In fact, the sign indicated that it would eventually lead up to a peak that looked over a beautiful vista. So, in my mind, it was not only too long but also too steep! I came up with the excuse that we would most certainly not have enough time to make the trip before the sun set. And we did not want to get caught in the park after it closed.

So we chose a path that another sign suggested. It would be a mile-long scenic walk. That seemed like just enough for me. I fortified myself with a good long drink from a convenient fountain. And then we began our journey.

Initially it was fascinating, mysterious, and glorious all at once. But after about half an hour, I began to notice the incline growing steeper and steeper. This was surprising since the path was supposed to be a full circle leading back to the parking lot where it started. But not to worry, we thought. How much farther could we go before a mile was up? Another half hour passed. Now we were walking straight uphill, and the cold water I had drunk was starting to make my stomach cramp. And, most disturbing, it was getting dark. Something was wrong, and we decided it had to have been that sign.

Not knowing where this road was leading and how long it would take to get there, we turned around, fully aware that we had over an hour's walk back to where we had started. We had no choice. And genuine forest-deep darkness was setting in. At least, I thought foolishly, going downhill would be easier. I did not realize how easy it would be to stumble in the darkness. Strange sounds started to surround us city folk. The faster we walked, the more we stumbled, and the louder the sounds became. And don't forget those cramps! Veering off into the woods somewhere to take care of them was definitely out of the question. The demons inside of me were less frightening than the unfamiliar ones I would run into off the path.

Finally, a light broke the darkness. A park ranger, who was nowhere near as happy to see us as we were to see him, called to us. As he began to lecture us about breaking the law by being in the park after dark, I asked him to hold his thought and point me in the direction of the nearest outhouse. He did. And when I exited, relieved in more ways than one, he was shaking his head and shining his light at the sign that had misled us. He apologized for those "darn hooligans" who evidently had been turning signs around to confuse people into walking in the wrong direction. He swore that he would catch them next time. I hoped he would.

I had expected to find God in the magnificence and beauty of those ancient trees. Instead, led the wrong way, I experienced an emptiness and the fear that went with it so strongly that it literally turned my stomach. If hell is the absence of God, a darkness filled with frightening noises, and being lost, this brief experience of purgatory was more than enough for me. I don't ever want to feel again the way I did that night, lost in Muir Woods.

sorry,
stranger

THINGS ARE BAD, SO WE PUSH GOD AWAY. WE push God away, and things get worse.

It had been a particularly stressful meeting. To begin with, the meeting was convened at a time and location guaranteed to get everyone but the convener stuck in traffic.

Unfortunately, I have an almost neurotic compulsion never to be late. So I try to set out exceptionally early, anticipating that I will encounter delays. On this occasion I was able to arrive just as the meeting was scheduled to begin, only to find that I was the first one there. So I sat patiently as the attendees came in, each one later than the other. And each of them proceeded to blame their tardiness on the traffic.

When the meeting finally got underway, it was apparent that no one but me had written up his or her preparatory notes as had been expected. So I found my work being hurriedly photocopied to be used as a starting point and then even more quickly torn apart by everyone at the meeting. This was convenient for them to do since they were bringing nothing practical or concrete to the table. The whole meeting was frustrating and, for me, a horrible waste of time. I left as soon as I could.

Trying to salvage at least some part of a wasted afternoon, I decided to pull into the large parking lot of a grocery store. My intent was quite simple: I wanted to park, run in, pick up some much-needed cat food and litter, and then head right home without getting caught in traffic again. That way I would have accomplished something by my trip.

I soon realized that my luck had not changed for the better. The parking lot appeared to be totally full. After a few frustrating minutes of driving around, I found a space. Even though I could see it was a tight fit, I managed to park and get out of my car. Once out, I noticed that the car next to mine on the passenger side was flush up against my car. So, nice guy that I am, I figured I should move my car to another space so that the owner of that car would be able to get into it. For a moment I actually prided myself on how thoughtfully—and Christian-like—I was responding to the situation.

But before I was able to get back into my car and execute my act of charity, the owner of the car I was blocking came up and started to scream at me.

Now this clearly was not something I needed after the meeting I had just been through. Still calm, I told her not to worry, that I was indeed planning on moving my car because I saw that I had boxed her in. She did not hear what I was saying. She threatened that if I did not move my car that very instant, she would open her car door as hard as she could and dent the side of my car.

Listening to this not-so-pleasant voice with its not-so-veiled threats, I noticed for the first time that the reason my car was close to hers and appeared to be in so narrow a space was that her car was not parked legally. Incredibly, she had parked in a fire lane, close to the last space, mine, probably with the hope that she wouldn't be ticketed or towed.

When I saw that and heard her continued threats, I snapped. Any further thoughts of a Christian response quickly dissolved. I heard myself outshouting her with some very colorful and imaginative expletives. On a roll, I then advised her that if she did not quiet down and move her illegally parked car that instant, she would lose both headlights to my shoe. I couldn't stop at that. I informed her that I had no intention of moving my car since it was in a perfectly legal space and that upon entering her car if she so much as touched my car, I would file an immediate lawsuit and block her from leaving until I had called the police on my cell phone. Mind you, I shouted all this in one breath, loud enough to be heard in the far reaches of the grocery store.

It worked. Realizing that she was in the presence of a crazed person, her demeanor changed. Without a sound, she slowly squeezed into her own car without touching mine, which was no easy task. Then she pulled away meekly, not even daring to give me a look as she left.

My initial euphoric reaction of both victory and vindication not only over her but also over the whole rotten day was rather short lived. I started to think about what might happen if she decided to come back with her husband or boyfriend while I was in the store shopping. They could do some serious damage to my car and speed away before I came out of the store. The possibility frightened me enough to prompt my quick departure without my even going into the store to do my shopping.

More than that, I realized what a terrible response to her I had chosen to make. It certainly was not Christian, nor remotely what Jesus would have done, if Jesus would have ever needed to buy cat food. I could not even justify it by blaming the bad day I was having. For all I knew, her day had been much worse than mine. And even if it hadn't been, there was no way I could view my behavior as remotely acceptable. In retrospect, I could see that the best thing to do would have been to just move

my car and avoid further confrontation with someone whose nerves were obviously already frayed. But
I had freely chosen to ignore that option. I could
argue that her actions brought me down to her level.
But the bottom line is that I am the only one respon-
sible for my behavior, which in this case was both
disrespectful and violent.

I'll probably never see this person again. But
I would still like to somehow let her know that I'm
truly sorry for how I responded to her. I am not usually out of control like that. In fact, most of the time
I'm a very nice and gentle person. If she was having
a bad day, I'm sorry that I made it worse. I hope I
didn't cause her to go home and kick her dog, or
worse, her husband. I'm sorry I brought more vio-
lence to her world and mine and pushed God away
in the process.

And I do hope that whenever she is in a
crowded grocery parking lot she finds a large—and
legal—space for her car.

Stories of God's Image

God's image dwells in all of us. It is part of the stuff of which we are made; it is reflected in our lives, however imperfectly. We need only look at one another with the eyes of faith. None among us are doll-like reproductions of some remote and aloof deity. Rather, we are the descendents—children—

"In a short time the world will no longer see me; but you will see me, because I live and you will live. On that day you will understand that I am in my Father and you in me and I in you."

~ JOHN 14:19–20

---

of God, carrying within us the unmistakable likeness of our loving God. A son and daughter might look like their father, even love like their mother, and so carry their parents with them wherever life takes them. Some even have the faith to see the beauty of God's presence where no one else is able to find it.

made in whose image and likeness?

I GREW UP WITH ONLY BROTHERS. CONSEQUENTLY, our house reflected a decidedly masculine environment no matter what Mom tried to do.

I remember when my cousin would come from New York State to visit us. The prospect of having a girl in the house to torment was thrilling beyond our wildest dreams. Hiding under her bed at night or jumping out of a closet or putting a rubber spider into her milk—anything we could do to elicit a girlish scream would absolutely delight us. My parents would finally notice that something was wrong when my poor cousin would sob uncontrollably before going to bed and jump at any unexpected sound. Then the fun would be over.

Looking back on it, I admit that we were terribly cruel. But all of it was really motivated out of ignorance. We just did not have a clue as to how to treat a girl in our midst. Our boorish actions were really attempts at affection, and in a strange way, they reflected our genuine care for her. We didn't know how else to communicate with her.

I recall how mixed up my own feelings became once when I was about eight years old and she was just nine. After I'd been playing nicely with her in the backyard and thoroughly enjoying myself, my cousin went inside to take a nap. Soon after, a gang of my guy friends came over and started making fun of me because, in the middle of baseballs and mitts and toy soldiers and racing cars, my cousin had dared to leave her favorite doll. So I joined them as they poked and kicked it and ran over it with the Tonka truck as though it were some sort of alien creature set down among us. I also recall getting into trouble because she cried when she saw how dirty and banged up her doll was.

I have to admit that from that time to the present I have learned nothing at all about dolls. When my brothers finally had children of their own, the cosmos played an ironic trick on the family: Only one son was born among all the daughters. Even then, I shied away from dolls as Christmas and birthday presents.

I walk into a toy store and am overwhelmed by all of the dolls and their incredible capabilities. Some of them talk, others walk, one even tumbles. You can feed some and change others. Many of them cry.

Once, in a parish Christmas pageant to which I was assigned, the plaster baby Jesus of the nativity set broke. So at the last minute we processed to the church's manger during midnight Mass with a con-scripted baby doll. To everyone's surprise, after the doll was set inside the crib it started to move its arms and legs. "Baby Stretches" was the name on the box from which we'd taken it. It almost became a holiday miracle. It scared me, that's for sure. We took the batteries out so it would just lie there like it was sup-posed to until after the Epiphany.

But Christmas and dolls do go together. Children carry their dolls everywhere on Christmas morning after opening their other gifts. The dolls go with them to church, to Grandma's house, and then to bed with them.

The marketing of dolls has become very important. At one time dolls were just for little girls. Then marketing made sure that dolls appealed to mothers as well, thus resulting in Barbie and Marie Osmond collectibles. And the price tag on some of them is amazing.

In an attempt to expand purchases to boys, as well as keep the demand high, a new—and for me, frightening—concept has developed. It came to my attention last Christmas when I saw a little girl hold-ing her new doll. The two of them caught my eye because the girl and the doll were wearing identical dresses and hats. The girl saw me looking at the doll, so she held it up proudly for me to see. I jumped back in shock. The doll not only was dressed like the girl but also had the same hair color and style, complexion, and eye color. This girl was carrying a miniature self. It was the zenith of reality-like dollness. It was also eerie. I was glad that at least the doll couldn't talk.

Later on Christmas morning, I saw this concept taken to another level. A little boy in blue pants and a red plaid shirt carried a doll dressed in exactly the same outfit, down to the shoes. The boy was proudly showing it to whoever wanted to see it, proclaiming, "I'm Johnny and so is this!" This doll was appealing to the narcissism that is in every child.

I am no traditionalist. Boys can and should play with dolls, and not just those G.I. Joe types. And girls should play with trucks. This is certainly a better approach to boys and girls than the one that prevailed when I was a boy. But I am a little worried that if these mirror-image dolls catch on, someone might order, as a gift for me, one that has a gray mustache, a droopy nose, and significant jowls and wears a black shirt with a white collar. The thought of a miniature me is downright frightening.

Critics complain that Barbie was an unreal image for most young girls to aspire to. She probably did little for a child's identity and sense of worth.

But, for lots of reasons, I am not sure that a doll that is a carbon copy of its owner is any healthier.

We often say that we are made in God's image. I don't think, however, that this means we are little doll-like reproductions of what God looks like. Being made in God's image means reflecting the majesty and the mystery that is part of the God who is at once unseen, unknowable, and yet familiar to each one of us in our own way. We are touched by the essence of God. Our bodies are just the package in which we happen to find ourselves today.

I suggest that we let children be creative once again. Dolls should return to being generic and simple, empty vessels of a sort, soft and huggable. Let the child's imagination and creativity and ability to dream give the doll vitality and life, personality and spirit. Then it will become infinitely more than just what it looks like. And we will be teaching our children that we are more than who we appear to be. That is, after all, how God made us, so that we could better find out how to mold ourselves into God's image, with God's grace.

a mother's love

DAD NEVER LET THE GROCERY STORE BE OPEN
on Sundays. "If you don't make enough money
Monday through Saturday," he would say, "you
might as well close down the business." Sundays
were really made for rest. That meant church first,
then a big pasta lunch, afternoon naps, and driving
back to the store in the evening to check that all the
refrigerators and freezers were working. As a family,
this was our usual routine.

On rare occasions, we'd all pile into Dad's
1955 Chrysler Windsor Deluxe and go for a ride.
Usually it would just be along the lakefront. Now
and then we would drive out to visit relatives in the
suburbs, where my brothers and I had to be on our
best behavior. More often than not, however, our
Sunday trips would be to the cemetery, where we
would visit the graves of my grandfather and my
sister, who had died before I was born.

Without the benefit of modern expressways, that trip was a long one, all the way out of the city and into the western suburbs. We drove there along beautiful boulevards. Not only were they the fastest and most direct routes available at the time, they were also the most scenic. And when I saw atop the tall building the giant Turtle Wax figure, like some lost monster from a cheap movie, I knew we were heading for Mt. Carmel Cemetery.

Driving along Washington Boulevard out of the city was very much like driving through a vaulted, leafy cathedral. Magnificent elm trees, reaching across the street and touching each other, formed a dappled ceiling high above us. And it went on like that for many miles.

I remember there being lots of conversation, often very loud as we tried to talk over the sound of the car radio. If I was given a window seat (I was often carsick), there would also be lots of my being pinched by my brothers, followed by my crying and then Mom telling us to sit still or else.

We never stopped to eat anywhere. Mom simply made sure that we had a good breakfast before we left home. The only scheduled stop we would make would be to pick up some plants or a ground cover to place on the graves. This stop also gave my brothers and me a chance to run and stretch our legs a bit.

I could tell when we were getting close to the cemetery. Dad would turn off the radio without saying a word, and Mom would take her rosary from her purse. The car would get very quiet. At the gated entrance, Dad would grip the steering wheel tightly and start to drive very slowly. Mom's eyes would well up with tears, and she would start to sniffle.

Dad had the route to the gravesite memorized even though the road twisted and turned its way through the cemetery. I would read the names on the tombstones, and since almost all of them were Italian, I thought, in the way small children draw conclusions, that only Italian people must die.

Mom would first walk up to Grandpa's grave and say a quiet prayer with tears in her eyes. But when she stepped over to my sister Annamaria's grave, where Annamaria's name was centered on a tombstone, our family name carved above in bigger, block letters, Mom would begin to sob openly.

Dad would go back to the car to get the flowers or the hoe or the watering can and then would busy himself clearing the area and planting. Mom would talk softly to herself through her tears. I felt very bad for her even though I never could hear exactly what she was saying no matter how close to her I stood. Sometimes I would just offer her my hand, not knowing what else I should do. She seemed to take it gratefully.

When Dad completed all of his tasks we knew that it was time for us to leave. At that point, however, there always seemed to be an awkward pause. We would never rush back to the car. Sometimes Dad and my brothers and I would be in the car and ready to go only to look up and see Mom still by the grave all by herself. Dad would wait patiently for her. As we finally began the drive home, the farther away from the cemetery we got, the lighter the mood would grow until the radio was finally turned on and we were back to normal.

Those memories are close to half a century old, but they remain with me as vivid as ever. Recently, as my mother was approaching her ninetieth birthday, she told me of a dream she'd just had. In it she was holding Annamaria in her arms. Dad was supposed to drive by in a car and pick them up. But he didn't come, so, holding her baby, she started to walk and got lost. In her dream she comforted her crying daughter and told her not to worry because Dad would eventually come for them. It was then, she told us, that she woke up feeling very sad. I had to ask her if it still hurt today as much as it did fifty-three years ago when Annamaria died. She responded softly by saying, "Sometimes more."

She still visits the graves at the cemetery, though not as often. And when she is there, she still cries. A mother's love never ends. Dad died a number of years ago. And he has not yet come for Mom. When he does, I am confident that Mom will once again be able to hold Annamaria in her arms. She has taught me that a mother's love mirrors God's love more than any other human experience. It transcends time and carries on into eternity.

When I need to feel that God is with me, especially in moments when I am doubting, I remember Mom's love for Annamaria and for me. And I believe.

dad and the hospital and me

MY DAD HAD A TREMENDOUS FEAR OF BEING A patient in a hospital, which, given the kind of patient he was when he was there, was clearly justified. His first stay was for prostate surgery. He was able to convince the doctors to discharge him early by promising to take all of the time necessary to heal at home. They believed him. They shouldn't have. When my uncle called from the grocery store complaining about everything that was going wrong, my dad used it as an excuse to rush out the door and back to the store, ignoring my mother's protestations. Within two days he was back in the hospital, bleeding and worse. He became virtually impotent; one could say that the store had literally stolen his manhood. The angry family doctor lectured him and told him that he would be lucky if his wife did not leave him. Lucky and blessed my father was.

His next stay in the hospital was for his gall bladder. He had an adverse reaction to the anesthetic after the surgery. The ICU staff was actually poised to give him alcohol intravenously, thinking that he was going into severe withdrawal. They refused to believe that my dad was only a moderate drinker—of wine with Sunday pasta and a beer with Saturday steak and not much else. During that period, when my dad's survival was touch and go, that same family doctor, like any good Italian, himself began to cry and say that all we could do was put it in God's hands. As a youngster, I remember thinking that this was an undoctorlike response. Dad was again blessed. He recovered just fine.

Late in life, bedeviled by a series of small strokes, Dad was hospitalized with increasing frequency. He also grew less steady on his feet. Once, while hospitalized, he had to be tied to his bed. This served a twofold purpose. It kept him from throwing his slippers at the unsuspecting nurses in frustration. And, more important, it kept him from getting out of the bed unaided and falling, something that had happened on numerous occasions.

I visited him one evening after he had been strapped down. More like a visiting chaplain than a concerned son, I took his hand, which was trapped in the restraints, and told him that I knew exactly how he felt. Well, in no uncertain terms he let me know that, having never been tied to a bed against my will, I had absolutely no idea how he felt. And he was right. So, fueled by his guilt, I was able to convince the nurses to untie him and that he would be good and not try to get out of bed without their help. My visit the next day was not a good one. He was tied down once again. He had tried to walk by himself to the bathroom and had fallen. In desperation he started promising me first new tires for my car and then a new car if I would sneak him out of bed and to home. I left with him angry at me. I felt rotten. But ultimately Dad was blessed. A few years later he would die in his own bed, at home, the way he wanted it.

A number of years later, at a time in my life when I was working eighteen hours a day, seven days a week, and fooling myself into believing that this pace was energizing me, I started to dream a lot about my dad. They were dreams of him when he was ill and in the hospital. Some would say they were premonitions. My lifestyle finally caught up with me, and I found myself flat on my back in a hospital bed, being told sternly not to leave it, as though that were possible with all the equipment to which I was wired holding me down.

I consciously tried to be a better patient than my father. So instead of arguing, I would ask questions—a lot of them—with the hope of wearing down the staff until they would just let me go home. Finally, an intern, despite what I had been told by every other doctor and nurse, saw nothing wrong with my getting up and sitting at the sink to partake of a luxury I desperately desired. So, careful not to unplug anything that might cause a nurse to come running into my room in a panic, I sat myself down in front of the steaming hot water with a fresh towel, a new blade in the razor, and some soothing lather.

Unfortunately, I could not see my own reflection in the mirror because my extended-wear contact lenses had been removed sometime during my arrival at the emergency room. Someone had brought me my old glasses, the ones I had put aside for an emergency and had not worn in years.

So that I could see what I was doing, I put on the old glasses, and everything stopped. It wasn't me that I saw looking back at me from the mirror. My hair was curled and matted down from many days of no shampooing. A week's growth of now-graying stubble covered my chin. My pallor was that of someone who was clearly sick. And my glasses had frames that were the same color and style my dad had worn his entire life. All of this together, looking right back at me, formed a clear portrait of my father. It was him I was looking at in the mirror, not myself.

All those dreams I had been having were not dreams of my father sick and dying in the hospital. I had been dreaming about myself all that time. It was as though something inside of me had been trying to warn me that there would be serious consequences if I did not slow down and take care of myself. I didn't listen, and so the son had become the father.

I don't know how long I stared at the reflection. My feelings changed from shock, to fear, to realization, and finally to a strange lightheartedness. I began to chuckle quietly. A concerned nurse came into the room and immediately put me back into bed without letting me finish the shave I hadn't really been able to start.

Well, Dad, I thought, lying there all hooked up, *now I guess I do know how you felt.* I also felt strangely at peace knowing that he was not just here for me at that moment, but that a real part of him was now a part of me. I knew that he had been blessed, and so now I felt blessed myself. Like father, like son. Made in his image. I understand better what that really means. So knowing that I am made in God's image makes me feel even more graced and blessed, thanks to Dad.

what's in a name?

I WAS NAMED, SIMPLY ENOUGH, AFTER AN UNCLE, unlike my four older siblings. My parents used up all of my grandparents' names with them. That took care of Annamaria, Joseph, Felix, and Anthony. But I had to be called something. While in many ways our family may have been considered strange by some, the names of my one sister and three brothers did not mean that I had one grandmother and three grandfathers. Conveniently, my brother Anthony was named for my maternal grandmother, Antonia. Some would say they shared other traits, but who am I to judge?

Since all the grandparents' names had been used up, there had been, I am told, some serious talk about naming me after my father. My dad had been named for the saint's feast day on which he was born. This practice was not uncommon if all the grandparents' names had been used up by older siblings and there were no other family names from which to choose or relatives to honor. That had been the case for my dad as well as for me. Dad's birthday fell on July 10, the feast day of an obscure martyr named Rufina. Since she was a woman, Dad's parents simply changed the name to its masculine form, Rufino. So, yes, my dad carried the same name as the Chianti wine wrapped in straw, the only other Rufino you are ever likely to run into.

So my dad liked the idea very much of having me named after him. It would have made him proud. But my mother rejected it outright. Over the years, the Americanization of his name led him to be called "Ruffo," even on his driver's license. My mother insisted that she didn't want her youngest son to have to respond every time a dog barked.

In retrospect, my dad's desire to have a junior is somewhat surprising. People often mistakenly called him Rufus, which doesn't sound Italian at all. I remember junk mail coming to the house for Rudolfo, Ruddo, Russo, and, my favorite, Fusso. Why he would have wanted to inflict that on me, I'll never know. My mother, thank God, prevailed. She soothed my father's ego by suggesting his older brother's name for me. And thus I was christened Dominic.

Every year in grammar school the sisters would ask me for which St. Dominic I had been named. I had two choices, the first being St. Dominic Savio, the good Italian teenager who was the patron saint of choirboys and juvenile delinquents. The other was St. Dominic the Preacher, to whom Mary had presented the rosary. Dominic the uncle, I learned early on, was not an acceptable response, since he was still alive and could not be counted among the community of saints yet.

I leaned away from Dominic Savio because the picture in our *Saints of the Day* coloring book made him look kind of wimpy, and I couldn't carry a tune and didn't carry a switchblade. So I chose Dominic the Preacher, since his feast day fell on August 4, just a few days before my own birthday. He was Spanish, not Italian, so it was a brave decision on my part.

When the church redid the Calendar of the Saints in the sixties, Dominic the Preacher's feast day was bumped to August 8, my birthday. Consequently everyone now thinks that I was named after the saint of the day and not my uncle. I'm here to set the record straight, although in many ways this is certainly better than someone thinking you were named after a legend like St. Christopher or a catacomb designation like St. Secundo. I count my blessings that we two Dominics are together on the eighth.

A while back, however, everything changed. I was idly thumbing through a copy of *Butler's Lives of the Saints* and came upon still another St. Dominic. He was called Dominic of the Causeway, and he is the patron saint of roads and tollgates. His story is very interesting.

It seems that, coincidentally, this Dominic desired to become a priest. But he was turned down by various religious communities because he was not able to meet their intellectual standards. (Here I would like to believe that the coincidences have ended.) So instead, he became a hermit and chose to live in a forest. Travelers making their way from one town to another through the forest were often set upon by robbers and brigands. Dominic saw this and was appalled. So he single-handedly built a road between the two towns, thus making travel safe for anyone and also securing a place for himself in the heavenly courts. The church celebrated holy brawn over holy intelligence in this rare case, at least consciously. How I wish the sisters from grammar school were around to ask me for which Dominic I was named.

My family name, Grassi, by the way, means "the Fat Ones." (Here, unfortunately, come those coincidences again.) Actually, in a small, poor town in Italy, to be so named was a compliment. To be fat meant to be prosperous and wealthy enough to have extra flesh on your bones. Evidently, they weren't aware of thyroid conditions. Those so named acknowledged it as a blessing and were pleased with the recognition.

Dominic, of course, translates very beautifully from the Latin to mean, "belonging to the Lord." So here I am, Dominic Grassi, the fat one who belongs to the Lord, a priest who celebrates his birthday on the feast of St. Dominic the Preacher but has an affinity to St. Dominic of the Causeway, who is a reminder to us all that we do not have to be smart to be a saint. But in reality I am simply named after my father's brother, who was also my godfather and was neither dumb nor fat.

Why do I get so excited by all of this? I just stop and think about what might have happened if I had been named Ruffo. And anyway, names just do not seem to carry that much weight anymore; witness the influx of Brads and Jeremys. Children are named after who is in style nowadays or are given any name that sounds good. I suppose we have to be called something to distinguish ourselves from each other. But since we are all God's children and made in God's image, our actions really are what will ultimately identify God's likeness in us.

the face
of god

IT HAS BEEN OVER A QUARTER OF A CENTURY
since she died. It's sad to say, but I cannot even begin
to remember her name. But her face, that face, and
what it still means to me today so many years later I
could never forget.

I was new to ministry back then. It was my
first assignment after my ordination. I was eager and
anxious and more than a little naïve. I don't remember much of those first days and months. But I do
remember that woman and the situations surrounding
her. One of my tasks was to bring holy communion to
the shut-ins. However, due to the racial change in the
community, there were no longer many elderly left
to visit.

The secretary called and told her that the
new, young priest would be coming by in the morning. I rang the woman's doorbell in her run-down
apartment complex. Through the crackling intercom

I identified myself. But she resolutely would not let me in. It took a phone call from the pastor whose voice she recognized for me to gain access to her small apartment.

Before I even stepped through the front door I knew that I was dealing with someone who was incredibly frightened. Again, I rang her buzzer and again she hesitated. Getting angry now and ready to leave, I was surprised when the hallway door finally clicked open. I went up the staircase to her apartment, muttering to myself that this should have been much easier than it was turning out to be. I could hear her fumbling with a number of locks, and then everything grew quiet. After an interminable moment I heard, "Well, are you coming in or not?" It was not a warm and inviting welcome.

I pushed open the door and walked into a small, well-kept apartment. An upright piano in the corner immediately caught my eye. Before I entered she had turned her back to me. As I began to introduce myself, she swung herself around to get a look at me. What I saw was unexpected and shocking. Even as I felt my stomach turning, I tried desperately to hide the surprise and revulsion that welled up inside me. I did not succeed.

She turned away. "I disgust you," she said softly. I tried to stammer a soothing reply. But, even to me, my words were hollow and weak. I could not stop looking at her face. After I'm not sure how long, she told me her story. She was a retired public-school music teacher. She had taught many generations of children to appreciate the beauty of music. After she retired she would occasionally earn some money as a substitute teacher.

Because many years earlier her mother had received a misdiagnosis, which caused her to be pronounced dead only to live to talk about it, this woman had developed a profound fear of doctors. So when she spilled some caustic permanent-wave solution in her eye while fixing her hair in preparation for a subbing job, she attempted to self-medicate the ensuing infection. Her efforts did not work. The infection grew worse. She sewed a patch, but the eye grew even worse. The infection spread and she stopped subbing. Eventually she stopped leaving her apartment as the infection spread even further. With no family to aid her, she began to rely on neighborhood children to do her shopping. They charged her twice what the food cost. Sometimes they took her money and never brought her anything in return.

So what I saw that first visit was a face half eaten away by infection. Her right eye had fallen into an open sore. A childhood filled with Vincent Price horror movies had not prepared me. I felt incredibly guilty for showing my feelings. So after I listened to her story I foolishly invited to take her to a doctor.

She proceeded to kick me right out of the apartment and said she would never let me in again if I mentioned taking her to a doctor.

So I would quietly bring her communion week after week and never refer to her face again. A new parishioner, a nurse, asked if anyone needed to be helped with regular visits. So one day I brought her along with me, and to my surprise, they got along well. Soon she was shopping for the woman and helping her keep her place clean. Having been warned not to make any suggestions of taking the woman to a doctor, the parishioner used her nursing skills to gently clean the woman's face and apply antibiotics. In return, the woman would play beautiful music on the piano for her, saying that it was the only gift she had to share.

One morning the nurse came and found the woman on the floor, unconscious. She called for an ambulance. Then she called me. The infection, not surprisingly, had spread to her brain. She did regain consciousness in the hospital. But she kept her good eye shut in anger when the nurse and I came to visit her. She felt that we had betrayed her trust. We had placed her against her will in a hospital, where she was surrounded by dreaded doctors. And there she died, angry with us until the end.

Only that nurse with her own little daughter attended the funeral. So instead of anyone delivering a homily, that good and generous nurse and I just sat and shared our reflections about the woman with the horrible face who made such beautiful music. I remember being angry. Where were all those people who she had helped to find the beauty and the awesomeness of the music locked up inside of them? Where were all those people with whom she had shared her gift of teaching? Where was anyone? Surely she had made a difference in someone's life.

And that is when the nurse told me that every time she looked at that horrible face, so disfigured, she saw the face of Jesus, the suffering face. And every time she listened to the woman play the piano, that poor woman was transformed into someone incredibly beautiful, reflecting the image of a loving God who held us all in a gentle embrace.

I had missed seeing that face of God. It was my loss. But that woman did not die alone. The nurse, who was sitting in the pew crying softly for someone who had grown very special to her—she had seen and celebrated the woman's beauty, God's beauty. And this mourner's presence was more than enough.

We have to be sure not to miss God's beauty and God's image. It is right there before our eyes, if we can only see beyond what our eyes are showing us.

Stories of God's Order

A troubled teenager chooses to jump from a car, a loved one nearly dies in front of his helpless family, and we are told to trust in God and not be afraid to smile no matter what might happen in life. How can this be? We need reminders that God's loving care envelops all of creation. We are never alone. So

"So do not worry; do not say, 'What are we to eat? What are we to drink? How are we to be clothed?' It is the pagans who set their hearts on all these things. Your heavenly father knows you need them all. Set your hearts on his kingdom first, and on his righteousness, and all these other things will be given you as well. So do not worry about tomorrow: tomorrow will take care of itself. Each day has enough trouble of its own."

~ MATTHEW 6:31–34

memories of long walks

to sacred shrines and

fireworks and thunderstorms help us recollect God's

order—enough, we hope, to allow us to believe

during difficult moments.

on being someone's last hope

COLLEGE YEARS SEEM FOR WHATEVER REASON TO accentuate all of our feelings. When we are down, we are lower than anyone could possibly imagine. When we are in love, no one could be more exquisitely lovestruck than we are. All of our emotions seem magnified. Thank God this happens when we are young, because it takes so much of our energy, much more than I would be capable of expending at this point in my life.

So there I was in seminary graduate school. I was young, I was Italian (which gave me that additional emotional dimension), and it was the sixties, when people were supposed to give free expression to all their feelings. All of this set me up for the story I'm about to share.

Midwinter in the first year of school, I received a call. It was from a court caseworker asking me to come to a meeting about a family I had known for a number of years. The youngest son, who was only seventeen, had been sentenced by a juvenile-court judge to regular and ongoing supervision and counseling because of his drug use. Since the family could not afford professional treatment, the caseworker suggested they talk to me. Surprisingly, the judge approved my meeting with the teen to fulfill the court's sentence.

As the caseworker privately confided to me that I clearly was this young man's last hope, my feelings of power and importance began to swell. I had never been anyone's last hope before, so the thought of being so important an influence in a person's life really caught my fancy. I did not for a moment think about the consequences of having absolutely no credentials or experience in counseling teens with drug problems. My limitless goodwill, my deep well of wisdom, and my awesome strength would be all I would need to set a life back on the right course and have this young man and his family forever grateful to me. As his last hope, I could not conceive of letting him down.

So we met at the caseworker's office. Tim was quiet, but that was because he didn't know what to expect. His parents looked worried. *Well, they just haven't seen me in action yet,* I thought. The caseworker appeared relieved. I can see now that it was probably because this would be one less file for him to worry about. So I did all the talking, more than an hour's worth. Clearly, everyone needed to be impressed. I thought that I was doing a masterful job of it.

I decided we would begin that very day. I would drive Tim home, with his parents in the backseat of the car listening to me, and the family would quickly be on its way to full recovery.

Driving down the highway, I continued to do all of the talking. Tim was quiet, as were his parents in the backseat. As I was talking on and on about the biweekly meetings I was going to schedule, Tim finally spoke up. It was just two words: "No way!" He then opened the car door and jumped out. We were going at least forty miles per hour. His mother screamed. His dad cursed. And I finally shut up.

Fortunately for Tim and for his parents, and to some extent for me, he landed in a freshly plowed snowbank. It softened his fall and kept him from rolling down the road. I stopped the car, paused, then threw it in reverse. Tim couldn't run. He had sprained his ankle severely, which, luckily for him, was his only injury. At the emergency room, the police came and took Tim into custody. He was ultimately placed in a youth detention center. I left the hospital in shock and pain, feeling as if I was the one who had just jumped from a fast-moving vehicle.

I decided that, right then and there, I needed some tender loving care. So I drove to a rectory to talk with a priest whose wisdom and insights I admired. He was also compassionate. I needed someone to tell me how exquisite was the pain I was feeling, a true martyr's pain.

He listened to the whole sad tale—from the moment I had become Tim's last hope until I saw him taken away, limping, by the police. Then I paused, assured that now was my time to start feeling better.

The priest took a long look at me and slowly shook his head. Then, to my shock, he roared, "How dare you—how dare you for even a moment—be so presumptuous as to think you could conceivably be anyone at all's last hope? How incredibly, selfishly prideful could you be? No wonder Tim chose to jump out of a car."

If I was in pain before his words, I now was so stunned that the only sound my mouth could produce was a barely audible "Ow!" Fr. Jerry softened a bit and went on to tell me more gently that the counselor had been wrong to suggest that I would be Tim's last hope and that I had been wrong to believe him.

Fr. Jerry helped me realize that no one is ever anyone's last hope. Sure, Tim was now in a difficult situation, and none of us knew how it would turn out. But the counselor, Tim's parents, and I—and, we could hope, Tim—needed to believe that God loved Tim, always had and always would. Tim would never be abandoned. Someone would be there for Tim—if not me, then someone else. And God would always be there for him. That's how God works.

That was a hard message to argue with. Fr. Jerry decided that I didn't need to feel better as much as I needed to learn a lesson. It was my turn to learn that, as pride-filled and foolish as I am, God still had plans for me to someday be someone's hope—not someone's last hope, but still someone's hope. God's plan and order for what he wants of me and all the Tims I will encounter in my life will be determined by God's working through me, not by any talent or abilities on my part. It was a good lesson to learn. I am sure that it has kept me many a time from jumping out of a fast-moving car and (figuratively and literally) others with me from doing it as well.

long walks and pilgrimages

"NONA IS GOING SHOPPING." THOSE MAGICAL words meant that I, a mere ten years old, would be called upon to serve as both translator and protector for my grandmother as she set out on her journey. Even at ten, I was as tall as she was short. Being her bodyguard made me feel really grown up. Besides, I could usually talk her into buying me some neat stuff that I otherwise would have no way of getting.

The only tradeoff (and I had already learned at the ripe old age of ten that just about everything in life involves a tradeoff) was that this elderly, slightly stooped Italian matriarch would inevitably walk me ragged. She had no use for buses or taxis or anything more mechanized than her old shopping cart with the bent and squeaky left wheel.

If I asked her, "Where are we going, Nona?" she would simply respond, "Somewhere," which was supposed to be answer enough for me. So every outing had a mysterious edge to it. I did know that whenever we went and whatever initial direction we took, we would always end up at the same place, the last stop before home. She always had this order to her journey. By then, despite all the treasures I had conned her into buying for me, I'd be exhausted, whiney, and not very appreciative.

I distinctly remember one spring morning when we hit the road. As usual, she walked briskly and quietly, with purpose and resolve. We had no time to spend on small talk of any kind. Also, I knew her well enough to have eaten a big breakfast, because we would never stop for a meal or even a substantial snack. At best I would convince her to buy me a candy bar or some fresh popcorn as we walked past the right shops.

Off we went one Saturday, heading west on Belmont Avenue. I figured that it couldn't be too bad a trek. Clearly we were headed for the Lincoln-Ashland shopping district. That meant stops at Wiebolt's for the fancy stuff and Goldblatt's for the bargains. Who knew what was on her list or would catch her fancy. It could be dish towels or a set of juice glasses or imported Christmas ornaments. Whatever she was looking for would slowly fill her cart. And, once home, she would carefully set the unopened or taped boxes on a shelf in the back of our cellar, to be brought out for use only if and when she approved.

I cannot remember what she purchased on that particular day. But I do remember registering surprise when, after shopping, we angled down Lincoln Avenue heading southeast rather than due east toward home. When Lincoln reached Clark Street, we turned straight south, a new and uncharted course for me. I could see that we were in for a long walk, so I asked Nona to buy me a "monster" magazine at a five-and-dime store. She looked at it and, seeing the scary pictures, muttered something about "diavola" (devil), but relented. At Chicago Avenue, which we reached an hour later, we headed east, stopping at Holy Name Cathedral. Whether she was just incredibly lucky or her timing was impeccable, I'm not sure. We entered just as Mass was beginning. I took the opportunity to rest my sore feet.

After Mass we headed north, toward home. But I knew that, as tired as I was and as she must have been, we had one more inevitable stop. Walking through beautiful Lincoln Park brought us to Columbus Hospital, where my brothers and I had been born. Not only was it a hospital founded by St. Francis Xavier Cabrini herself, it was also the location where God chose to call her to her final reward. The room where she died has been preserved as a shrine.

Everything in the room was old looking to me and covered in plastic—an Italian tradition. An oil painting of Mother Cabrini dominated the scene. A lit candle and the hushed voices assured me that we were in a holy and sacred place.

Nona would speak in Italian with some of Mother Cabrini's sisters. The Missionary Sisters of the Sacred Heart worked as nurses and administrators at the hospital. They could be alternately gentle and severe. There was the little nun who sneaked an ice-cream snack to my brother after his back surgery. But there was also my mother's situation. Mom told me that when she yelled out in pain during her contractions just before I was born, one of the attending sisters told her to be quiet, that she had had her fun, and now she had to pay the price. Mother Cabrini herself, I am told, could be both kind and tough, a good combination for a builder and a saint.

I do not know what my grandmother would say about me to the various sisters in charge of the shrine, but they would always smile and give me a handful of holy cards, prayer booklets, medals, rosaries, and pins. Some of the material was in English; much of it was in Italian. My dresser drawer at home became filled with these treasures because I didn't know what to do with all of them. I noticed that as we would leave the hospital, Nona would allow herself a little self-satisfied smile, something that rarely appeared on her face.

She had, it would seem, taken a mere shopping trip, a long walk, and turned it into something

sacred. Because of this last, necessary stop, her trip
would become a true pilgrimage, a realization of
the age-old custom coursing through her veins.
That made her feel good about the day and allowed
her to justify what she had done. She was keeping
the right order, an order that had been in place
for generations.

She would, at this point, pick up the pace.
After the visit to the shrine, the last half hour of the
walk home was almost a trot. Once in the house,
Nona would put everything away without a word.
My mother would have to sneak a look later. Nona
would sit down to dinner and just shake her head
as I showed everyone the neat stuff I had gotten,
including the religious materials from the shrine.
I would make sure to thank her again for all of it. It
would only be a matter of time until our next trip.

Since Chaucer's time, the pilgrimage has been
a popular religious practice in Europe, part of the
order and fabric of society. Not so here in our culture.
Perhaps this is because we do not have a whole lot of
sacred sites or traditions or heritages to celebrate. It's
a shame. I am glad Nona kept the tradition alive for
me to experience. Each spring, as the weather warms
around me, I look for someplace special to visit. It
puts order into my life, sacred order, God's order. It is
good for both my body and soul, and is a nice trib-
ute to Nona, the pilgrim.

fireworks

JULY IS THE MONTH THAT AMERICANS MOST associate with fireworks. Fireworks have become so much a part of our patriotic celebrations that many among us probably believe that they are uniquely an American invention, their ancient Chinese roots and the current expertise of Italians ignored.

In the small town where my parents spent their youth in southern Italy's rocky hills, I discovered that fireworks were indeed used for other celebrations, in this case to celebrate the feast day of the town of Alberobello's patron saints. I also began a journey of discovery as to how God's loving order of creation is mirrored in beauty, such as what could be seen in a fireworks display.

The night before the actual feast-day activities, I was dragged, admittedly against my will, to a remote hillside outside of town where two different pyrotechnic firms would compete to be selected as the official fireworks provider for the feast of Saints Cosmos and Damian, to be celebrated the next night. The competition was scheduled to begin at midnight, for some inexplicable reason long since buried in tradition and, of course, never challenged.

Unlike the Italians from whom I descended, I arrived at the designated viewing area on time despite the protestations of my cousins from the town, who went with me. Not surprisingly, our family was the first there. Munching on mortadella and provolone sandwiches, we watched and waited as the crowd slowly gathered, some on bicycles and most in their little Fiats. We kept waiting. We ate more. And we continued to wait until 12:43, when two rockets screeched into the air without apology or warning and burst into light, exploding with a thunderous roar. Then we heard nothing at all for at least ten minutes except for the barking of hundreds of farm dogs awakened by the loud blast. That just couldn't be the extent of the competition, could it? In the cold, I wasn't too sure.

At this point I was ready to go back to the hotel and my warm bed. The hotel's proprietor had thoughtfully placed two twin beds side by side and covered them both with one king-sized sheet so that the visiting priest would have a grand bed in which to sleep. Nice sentiment, but the slat running down the middle kept waking me up as I rolled down into it throughout the night.

Now, as I sat groggily on the dark hillside, the real show began. It was the most phenomenal show of fireworks that I have ever experienced. Each company had one half hour to impress the judges. Both presentations left me awestruck and, at least temporarily, a little deafened. Never before and never since have I witnessed such an incredible spectacle of light and color and sound produced by human hands.

A few years ago I found myself on an airplane heading back to Chicago from Washington, D.C., on the evening of the Fourth of July. I was mightily disappointed that I would have to miss the festivities in our nation's capital. I had no idea how memorable the flight would be.

Initially we were flying through absolutely clear skies. As darkness approached, from my window I began to observe town after small town, villages, and urban centers, all of them setting off their holiday fireworks. Everyone on the airplane seemed struck by the beauty and the symbolism of what we were seeing from such a special vantage point. Given the day, the time of our flight, and the weather conditions, we sensed that this was a once-in-a-lifetime experience for us. One passenger even asked loud enough for everyone to hear what could possibly be a more beautiful sight to see.

The flight proceeded toward an oncoming cold front. Off in the distance I could see massive thunderheads rising thousands of feet into the sky where the cold air was colliding with the warm. Clearly some parts of the country were becoming too wet to have any kind of fireworks show or even an outdoor celebration.

Lightning began to flash inside the giant, rolling masses of clouds. Sharp bolts pierced through them dramatically, the likes of which I had seen only in comic books and my own imagination. It was all an incredible sight to view. The quiet on the plane reminded me of the opening line of the hymn: "Let all mortal flesh keep silent."

The seat-belt sign went on, and the captain announced that he would try to fly up over the worst part of the storm and turbulence. The ride grew bumpy. And what made it frightening was the envelope of gray darkness that closed in around us as we were being tossed about.

But suddenly, we broke through. Overhead the black sky was brilliant with the brightest of stars. And below was God's own fireworks display in the clouds, more awesome than anything human hands could create. Once again I felt that I was observing something special, a Fourth of July spectacle that I would never forget and a glimpse of the order in which God has placed us.

For me the sight of all that beauty and the fierce power of nature was a clear reflection of God's ordered creation, at once majestic and mysterious and strong. Our frail attempts to reproduce it, no matter how well done, are just a shadow of God's presence, a mere reflection of a much greater reality. And it seemed to answer that one passenger's question: What could possibly be a more beautiful sight to see?

Because of these experiences, I find myself enjoying Independence Day celebrations and any excuse for fireworks wherever I get to see them, in a big city or a small town, over the lake or in a baseball park. They inevitably remind me of a special night on the side of a hill in southern Italy, when I began to see more than I expected to see, on many levels. And, more important, they remind me of an even more special night on an airplane, flying home, when a miracle occurred and I realized how beautifully God has ordered creation.

fear of smiling

I NOTICED IT AT THE HOMETOWN FEAST-DAY celebration in Alberobello, the day after the fireworks. It was evening, when husbands and wives, boyfriends and girlfriends promenaded through the little Italian town's square together, arm in arm. The men were all dressed in suits, some so old that they were shiny—both the men and their suits. The women over forty all wore black dresses decorated at most with a pin or a gold chain. Younger couples dressed in the latest style from the States—jeans and T-shirts interchangeable between the sexes. The men led the women around almost as though they were showing off possessions. They smiled proudly and broadly, their gazes looking over the expressions on everyone else's faces. The women, on the other hand, were solemn. Not one of them wore a smile to complement her Sunday best. Their eyes darted furtively from left to right as they checked everything out.

They reminded me of pictures from our family album, pictures of my grandmother, who seldom had a smile on her face. I remembered other elderly relatives who wore that same permanent frown. Since no one around us spoke any English, I was comfortable in asking my mother why all of the women looked liked Nona and why none of them were smiling, at least none of the older ones.

She said simply that they were afraid.

"Afraid of what?"

"Mal occhia," my mother responded, "the evil eye!"

I was incredulous. Mom explained to me that if they looked too happy or satisfied, someone might put a curse on them out of jealousy. So they could not afford the risk of smiling. Clearly the men did not put much stock in such ancient superstition as they paraded the women proudly around town.

Superstitions die hard. This one may have dated back to pre-Christian roots and crossed the Atlantic with my grandmother and her generation. I thought, *How unsophisticated, how ignorant, mindlessly juvenile, and just silly.* I should have asked myself how many of these superstitions course through my blood generations later. Much more, I'm sure, than I would like to believe.

There *is* that part of me that gets a little uncomfortable when things start to go too well.

There is that streak of fatalism that rears its ugly head at unexpected moments. Sometimes when the sun is shining I find myself looking for a cloud off in the horizon somewhere. Do I deserve to be so happy? Why is life going so right for me? What is God really setting me up for? These are irrational questions, but real nonetheless. And often they are reinforced by life's ebbing and flowing.

Tonight, for example, I came home from a delightful evening of sharing my stories with a receptive audience in a warm and comfortable setting. It was an uplifting and, at the same time, humbling experience for me. Driving home on that cool and beautiful early autumn evening, I was unable to savor the grace of the few hours I had just experienced. Instead, a sense of foreboding and doom washed over me. *I am feeling too good. Something has to happen to knock me down, put me in my place.* It wasn't my fear of the evil eye. To me, this is just how life is, how God insists life must be.

And sure enough, I came home to a note warning me that a parishioner who was coming to Mass the next morning was very unhappy about a decision I had made and that I was going to hear about it. *See, that's what I get for letting myself enjoy this evening so much. I should have known better. I probably won't sleep well tonight because I'll be playing out different scenarios over and over in my mind, none of them terribly pleasant. I knew that I should never have let myself feel so good.*

I really have no idea what is going to happen tomorrow. The best-case scenario is that everything will be just fine. And the very worst that might happen won't be anything I can't handle. No matter what the situation, it really has no connection to the wonderful night I just had. Why spoil it? Why should I, like those hometown Italian women, be afraid of smiling?

Too often we do not let God be God. We are not puppets on a string that God chooses to pull benevolently so that we can soar and dance or malevolently so that we fall flat on our faces. But neither are we solitary bits of created matter left to float alone in an empty universe untouched by God's love and grace.

I have to believe that there is order to God's creation. There are reasons for and meaning to what happens in life; some of it we can control, and some of it happens quite by accident. Too often we make demands on God that are not fair, and we ask God to give us answers to questions for which there are no answers. We try to be sophisticated in our denial of the role that God does play in our lives. At the same time, we do not realize how primitive we are in our fears of being under God's thumb because of everything we have done or have even thought of doing.

When we think about it, it really does make more sense to simply smile when we are happy, cry when we are sad, whimper when we are frightened, and laugh out loud when something strikes us as funny. We need to admit that God's order often appears to us as disorder, that good times are as often followed by even better times as they are by bad times, and that the bad times seldom have anything to do with what has just proceeded them.

Jesus said that we should let tomorrow take care of itself. Like the birds of the air, we do not need to worry about it because whatever will happen in our future will include God's order. And God's order imparts God's love for us, which will never be taken away. We really do need to remember and believe that the love of God will always be there for us, especially when the chips are down and also when life is going so great for us that we cannot help but grin from ear to ear.

sliced any
other way

"NO MATTER HOW YOU SLICE THE BALONEY," MY dad once said to me, "it is still baloney. But prosciutto you have to slice paper thin or it is nothing at all." Then he gave me a wise look. I confess that as a child I had no idea what he was talking about. But since he was a man of very few words, I realized that this must be some kind of meaningful message. In any case, I loved to sneak back into the meat department before we locked up the grocery store at night and slice the prosciutto paper thin into my eager hand. It was and remains food from the heavens.

It took almost half a century for me to begin to understand what Dad was trying to say to me. And it happened when my oldest brother nearly lost his life.

A diet that centered around double Whopper cheeseburgers, forty years of a militant smoking habit of three packs of cigarettes a day, along with a change in lifestyle brought about by his retirement from a high-pressure government job left my brother Joe wounded physically, emotionally, and, I would venture to say, spiritually. All the signs were there, but we saw them only in retrospect. At his retirement party he looked worn out and run down. His trips back home to the Midwest grew more infrequent. He openly complained about anxiety attacks that were so bad that he hadn't slept in a bed for a long time, preferring instead to doze off at the kitchen table.

At one point, after receiving a phone call from a concerned friend, I flew out east and got Joe to his doctor. I felt more than a little self-satisfied about my dramatic intervention. But we were both fooling ourselves. He missed coming home for family anniversaries and weddings and even to see our seriously ill mother. Finally we insisted on a preholiday visit.

He didn't want to fly. So Phil, another brother, took a plane out east and then drove back to Chicago with him. He looked worse than any of us could have imagined. He walked with difficulty and sat hunched over like an old man. His smoking-induced cough was now chronic. He was plagued with anxiety attacks virtually every day. He would nod off constantly with a cigarette in his hand while he ate or rode in a car. I thought he was probably overmedicating himself since he was adding antihistamines and cough medicine to his prescription medications.

After seeing him, my brothers and I decided that we would not let him return home before he saw a doctor here with us. We decided to wait until the night before he was scheduled to leave to make our demands known. We were uncertain how he would respond. If he refused, we would let him go home by himself and no longer support his rationalizations.

Two days prior to that scheduled intervention, I drove him to spend a night with Mom. Her senior complex had guest rooms available. I thought that maybe she could convince him to get some help. Twice in the car he fell so quickly and deeply asleep that he lurched forward and nearly knocked my car out of gear by hitting the shift column. I drove faster, so much faster that I was stopped and issued a speeding ticket.

When Mom saw him, her knees nearly buckled in shock. When I got her alone, I assured her that we were going to get him to a doctor in two days. I left them together and drove home. Not more than an hour after I returned home, Mom called me. Joe was really sick and needed to see a doctor immediately, not in two days. It takes a mother to see things as they really are. I called my other brothers, but she called me again. Joe was falling out of the chair. So I told her to call 911. She chose to wait for Phil, who had called her on his way to her building. He would get Joe to the emergency room. Now semiconscious, my brother Joe lay with his head cradled in his mother's arms. She looked up to God and with both fear and anger shouted, "Did you send him to die in my arms?"

After he arrived at the emergency room, a doctor declared him, in not-so-medical terms, "a train wreck." He was placed in intensive care, where during the night he stopped breathing. He was put on a respirator, and because I had power of attorney, I was called to come to the hospital immediately. With the support of my other brothers, I had to make some choices. Would he be able to breathe if and when the respirator was taken off? What would we decide if he couldn't? His lungs were so damaged and his carbon-monoxide levels were so high that he could easily die. He had not been overmedicating himself. He was passing out from the lack of oxygen to his brain. Pneumonia had brought his condition to this acutely critical stage. He was much sicker than we had wanted to believe.

Fortunately, when Joe was taken off the respirator, he was able to breathe on his own. Antibiotics would clear the pneumonia. He would have no choice but to stop smoking, lose considerable weight, and use oxygen constantly with the hope that pulmonary therapy might eventually make him less dependent on the tanks and pumps. With the oxygen came relief from the anxiety attacks. They most likely were brought on by his inability to breathe. He is now able to sleep in a bed. He sits up and walks straight. He is, ironically, both damaged and better at the same time.

If he had not come for a visit when he did, someone would have found him alone and dead in his home out east. If he had not gone to visit Mom, he would have been all alone in his room in the rectory and probably would have passed out, never to wake again. It is obvious that his visit to Chicago was at the right time and that the visit to Mom was at the right time as well. With any other scenario he most certainly would have been dead.

Chance? I doubt it. If the situation had been sliced any other way, my brother would be gone now. For some reason, God's reason, it wasn't meant to be. So all the right components came together. Joe remembers nothing about being at Mom's place except for the vague image of her holding his head in her hands and how good and right that felt to him. It *was* good and right. It was what was supposed to be because that is how God works. It couldn't have been sliced any thinner. We can plainly see God's hand in what happened during those crucial, short hours. Now what will happen is up to my brother. God has done God's part.

Stories of **God's Word**

Listen. It is by hearing God's Word that we so often
find ourselves bumping into God. Those are
moments of grace. God speaks to us in so many and
varied ways. Our own human experiences can help
make Scripture, God's Word, alive and vital to us.
God speaks of love and forgiveness, even when our

> "But happy are your eyes because they see, your ears because they hear! I tell you solemnly, many prophets and holy men longed to see what you see, and never saw it; to hear what you hear, and never heard it."

~ **MATTHEW 13:16–17**

---

own voices can reflect only our limitations and sinfulness. And so God gives us signs of being present with us in parents who put up with us and in friends who eat our food. In countless, simple, yet marvelous ways, God's Word flows and pours into us like a fountain. We need only be open and listening.

what
sign?

I DO NOT CARE HOW FASHIONABLE IT IS THESE
days to look back on the early seventies and charac-
terize them as immature, unrealistic, hedonistic,
uncontrollable, or any other adjective with which
you might negatively label that time. For me and, I
am sure, many others who reveled in their first pair
of bell-bottom jeans, decked themselves out with
more beads around their necks than a Sister of Mercy
had on her old religious habit, and wore out the
track "Both Sides Now" on Judy Collins's album,
those years were nothing short of magical.

For some of us free spirits there couldn't have
been a more exciting time to be in a seminary, as
rules and regulations and traditions came tumbling
down around us like the walls of Jericho and new
structures had not yet been put into place. That
process would take a few years. So in that creative
vacuum we had the freedom to experiment with

programs of our own design, both in study and formation. We had a "groovy time," while I'm sure we were driving those who tried to work with and teach us absolutely crazy. I need to thank them now, publicly, for all their patience with us and the trust they ultimately placed in us. They were the best faculty a seminary could have.

In the wildest of those days, three of my closest friends and I somehow obtained permission to move into a ramshackle house more than ten miles away from the seminary campus, work in a local parish, and commute back for classes, prayer, and formational activities. In retrospect, it's clear that how that got approved, even in those days, was a miracle in itself. Nothing like that has happened at any other time in the history of the seminary. Let it be noted that all four of us did get ordained, so it was not a bad experiment. One even has become a bishop. But so his career does not stall, I'll refrain from mentioning him by name. These days, alas, are no longer the seventies.

In any case, we rented that big old house, which had a storefront attached to it with the intention of turning it into a parish teen drop-in center. That would be our ministry and work when we weren't in classes at the seminary. Unfortunately, the house left much to be desired. The plumbing leaked. The boiler was bad. Nails that stuck out of the floors would cause puncture wounds. It took us two hours to move in and two days to clean the bathrooms. In short, the place was perfect for us.

How did we pay for it? Two of us spent the summer doing road construction and praying for rain. Another was an orderly on the psychiatric ward of a local hospital, which was great training for being a pastor. And the future bishop "palletized" (his word) roof shingles in a manufacturing plant that later became noted for being one of the biggest polluters of Lake Michigan. We pooled our resources for the rent and lived on fifteen-cent frozen pot pies and parishioners' generosity. The house was cheap because its owner, a local real-estate baron named Bud, who owned more slum land than a character from Dickens, would not give us a lease. He rented to us monthly with the hope of eventually selling the property out from under us.

After all the work we did to clean up the place, we surely did not want that to happen. So one night, after a few bottles of Boone's Farm Strawberry Wine, we decided to take down the For Sale sign on which his name and phone number were painted in two-foot-high letters and numbers. We turned it over and painted our own sign welcoming everyone to St. Joseph Parish Teen Drop-In Center. We proudly rehung our revised sign and were really in business. It worked. The teens came in droves.

Shortly after this project, on a warm Saturday morning, we got a phone call. Bud the owner was coming by to see us. He had driven by the house the night before, an unusual occurrence, and did not see his For Sale sign. Before he arrived we quickly took ours (his) down and hid it in the garage, fearing that he would realize what we had done.

Now, Bud never did like us. In his mind we were just an interracial group of long-haired hippies. But our rent checks were better than no revenue from an empty building. He really didn't want to believe that we didn't know where his sign was. So he kept looking and finally decided that the wind must have knocked it down. We shrugged, feigning ignorance. Then Bud decided that maybe someone had placed the fallen sign in the garage.

We didn't panic. Two of the guys, without exchanging a word, ran to the garage ahead of him while the other two of us kept Bud busy by offering him a cigar. We made sure his back was to the store-front's picture window as they carried his (our) sign past it down the block to a weedy empty lot.

Just as Bud noticed that two of us were missing and began to get suspicious, they calmly walked in through the front door, their task completed. Bud asked them if they knew anything about the sign. The one who was to become a bishop looked at him with total innocence and asked, "What sign?" At that moment I knew he could go far in the church. We followed silently as Bud checked the garage and finally left, muttering to himself.

After a really good laugh, we boldly put the sign (our side up, not his) back in the yard for all to see, where it remained until we moved out two years later. Bud wouldn't be back to our part of town for a while. We knew it was safe. And we experienced what it meant to "beat the man."

Our words aren't always God's Word, but sometimes God has no choice but to use us and our words to communicate his wonderful and sometimes mysterious message. On some occasions God even turns our words around and writes a message on the back. At these moments we can search for our words, but they will be nowhere to be found. Like Bud, we'll never know where they went. But we are used in God's way for a much better purpose—to communicate God's message. There really isn't much we can do but let it happen. At that moment our faith becomes part of God's message.

sign language

LET ME BEGIN BY STATING CLEARLY THAT I'M not proud of what I'm about to relate. My actions were wrong, and I was without excuse. I hope that, in some way, the telling of this story can serve as an apology. And to those who argue further that it is wrong for me to even share what I did, I have to disagree. But I do offer these preceding words as a warning to anyone who might be easily scandalized to go no farther. I am going to bet that most of you are still with me. So, no complaining afterwards!

It began on a typical Sunday morning. I was very new at the art of preaching. Since it was so many years ago, I cannot honestly say if my words were dramatic or meaningful or effective. I have no recollection of what images or stories I used. I only vaguely recall that the message of my homily was that we are all called to share God's love with each other and that we need to see God's presence in everyone and so treat them with respect and love. I probably couched it all in the theological jargon I had just learned in the seminary.

My work completed for the day, I hopped into my car and headed home for pasta dinner with the family. It was tradition for us to gather every Sunday at my parents' house from wherever we may have been living at the time. It was rare that any of us missed dinner without good reason. Seldom did the meal even begin after 1:00 P.M. For me that was proving to be very problematic, because my mother would serve the pasta when it was ready—she didn't wait for stragglers. She knew that pasta was infinitely better when eaten fresh. In addition, latecomers risked missing the choicest meatballs and the meatiest oxtails, which had been cooked in the tomato sauce. It took me years to train my mother, who eventually learned to wait for my brothers' families because of their children, to afford me the same consideration because of my Sunday sacramental commitments.

But on this particular day, in the years before Mom waited for us, I was in quite a hurry to get from the southwest side of the city to the near north side, where my parents lived. Heading east on Seventy-sixth Street, I found myself trapped behind a car that was moving much too slowly. In my growing impatience, I tapped my car's horn. That had no effect. So I flashed my headlights, but that made no difference either. I was stuck, knowing that at that moment across the city, a boiling pot of pasta was al dente almost to the point of no return. I grew from agitated to angry. Nothing should be allowed to get in the way of something as important as Sunday pasta.

Finally, I just leaned on my car horn. An opportunity to pass appeared at last, and I went around the slow-moving vehicle. That should have been victory enough. But not for me, not then. Years before the term *road rage* was invented, I gave into temptation. As I went around the car that had become the source of all my frustrations, I raised the middle finger of my right hand in what can only delicately be described as the universal sign of contempt. I had a message to communicate, and at that moment this sign was the most satisfying way to do it.

Imagine my surprise, horror, and then profound embarrassment when I realized that the elderly couple in the car toward which I was directing all my anger were parishioners who had just told me a few moments before how beautifully my sermon on God's love and our need to love and respect one another had touched them. Their looks of total disbelief and shock let me know that they recognized me behind the gesture. Of course, my feeble attempt to make that gesture appear to be a friendly wave of the hand failed miserably. Not much was left to do but speed off with a much-deflated appetite.

I dreaded the following Sunday. I avoided them studiously until my internship at the parish was over. I never said anything to them, and they never commented about it to me or, as far as I know, to my supervisors.

What I did was simply wrong. There are no acceptable excuses. I was wrong not just because I happened to get caught. I was wrong because I chose not to practice the Word of God that I had preached just a few minutes earlier.

I did learn a valuable lesson from this incident. I learned that my words, even those I preach, are nowhere near as important as my actions. It is much too easy to preach someone else's message, one that we are not trying to live out ourselves, one that we divorce from our own actions. Instead, each one of us is called to preach, mirror, and live out God's words in our lives. And that simply can't be done in a few minutes on a Sunday in church. We are called to do it in the everyday stuff of life, and that means even when the pasta might get cold on the plate waiting for us. We help others recognize God through God's Word, which we live out even if we are not expecting to recognize the people to whom we are responding.

It has been said that God's Word is often a two-edged sword. It is indeed, and it has a very sharp blade. If we are not careful, like I wasn't that

Sunday afternoon, we will cut ourselves on it very easily.

coins and fountains

MY FAMILY HAS SOME VERY SILLY PICTURES THAT were taken when we all journeyed to Rome a few years ago. In them, we are standing with our backs to the beautiful Trevi Fountain. It almost looks as if we are waving at the camera when, in fact, we were tossing coins over our shoulders, just like in the fifties movie, to ensure that someday we would come back to the Eternal City. Even though many tourists take part in the ritual of throwing coins into the Trevi Fountain, no one has ever been able to explain to me how the custom started. And, come to think of it, no one seems to know where all those tossed coins go.

Unfortunately, those snapshots aren't capable of capturing the awesome beauty of the fountain, the almost magical sound of its rushing waters, and the unique smell and feel of the windswept mist. Like all of Italy, the Trevi Fountain must be experienced in person in order to be truly appreciated.

I have often wondered where the Italians' love of fountains originated. Perhaps it started with the Romans and their system of aqueducts and baths with those elaborate displays of flowing water. But now, many centuries later and an ocean away, it seems that many Italian Americans continue this tradition, setting up fountains large and small in their gardens, somewhere between the tomatoes and the roses. That is certainly the case with my own brothers. All three of them have little statuettes in their backyards dribbling recycled pumped water.

I am proud to say that I have topped all of them. Shortly after my arrival as pastor, I led the parish community in building a small park on the vacant land behind our beautiful twin-spired church, creating a space that would rival many old-country piazzas. I insisted that the architect include a large fountain as the centerpiece. People thought I was crazy and predicted it would cause more problems than it was worth. The original design called for an elaborate Gothic creation from England, elegant and impressive. But when we were informed of a strike at the manufacturing plant that could cause a year's delay and would double the price of the fountain, we reluctantly settled for a less ambitious structure.

So, after the trees and shrubbery were planted, the cement poured, the bricks laid, and the benches installed, the final touch was the unveiling of a two-tiered fountain topped with a cement pineapple out of which water cascaded with perfect symmetry over each level to the larger basin and was then pumped through again. The sounds were soothing and inviting, and the pineapple, we were told, was a symbol of welcome and hospitality.

How could anything so simple and nice become a source of so many problems? I don't know, but it very rapidly did. The first day the water flowed, one of our neighborhood street people decided to squirt some liquid detergent into it so that he could wash his clothes. He quickly ran off, totally naked, as the suds enveloped his clothes and soon covered the entire park, threatening to swallow a three-year-old in the process. It took our janitor the entire afternoon to drain the fountain and render it suds-free.

The very next week, as I drove my car around the corner and was admiring the park's beauty, I almost crashed into a stop sign when I saw the beautiful fountain tumbled over on its side like an ancient Roman ruin, all eight hundred pounds of it, water gushing everywhere. Neighbors informed me that it had just happened during the school's recess. Children had been playing and leaning on it, and it fell over onto a child's ankle. I've been told that I became so agitated at the sight of the disaster that I ran into school and demanded that the child who knocked it over and the teacher who was in charge of recess at the time see me immediately. I am told that I never even asked about the condition of the child upon whom the fountain had fallen.

After that episode, the foundation was reinforced with steel piping and additional concrete. It has toppled over only once or twice since then. I am learning, begrudgingly, to live with that as a regular possibility. We've also gone through a number of concrete pineapples. They appear to be very tempting to lop off with a baseball bat.

I find it very interesting that people seem compelled to toss their loose change into fountains for good luck or to make a wish, not only in Rome but also here in Chicago, and probably just about everywhere. Coins are always settled at the bottom of our fountain under the murky water in which pigeons have washed themselves and into which dogs have jumped to cool off.

During the ten years that the fountain has been flowing, we've not removed a single penny. Every day money gets tossed into it, and every day someone takes the coins out. It could be neighborhood children. More often than not, the street people are accused. I won't pass judgment. During my seminary years I would accompany my classmates who smoked to the Lourdes Grotto, which was across from our residence hall at the seminary. On Sunday evenings after the visitors had left, my classmates would fish out enough change for the cigarette machine. I'd search around for a quarter for a soda. It didn't seem wrong at the time, just expedient.

These fountains are to me small representations of how we respond to all that pours out from the word of God into our hearts. Some of us, in our gratitude, toss something back into the fountain. And some of us take from it in need. No matter what we do, it keeps flowing and flowing. God's Word never ends, and we can't change a thing, not here in a church park or in a backyard or even in Rome. God's Word is a grace that keeps on flowing.

an almost empty feast

SILENT AUCTIONS HAVE BECOME THE RAGE AT
fund-raisers these days. Potential donators walk
around table after table signing and re-signing their
names until they become quite literally dizzy from it
all. The more unique the items or services offered, the
more frenzied the bidding becomes, especially during
the final minutes and seconds. There is usually a lot
of good-natured elbowing, but also a little meaningful
pushing in attempts to be the final signature on the
bidding sheet before the time runs out. And sometimes, when people are bidding seriously on more
than one prize, there is a lot of running around the
tables as well.

Being neither rich nor well connected, I have
nevertheless found an item that I can contribute to
various causes. I offer to come to the winning bid-
der's house, or they can come to my rectory, and I
will prepare for a party of four a gourmet Italian

meal, an eight-course feast starting with antipasto
and ending with dessert. I jokingly let it be known
that any winning bid that comes in at under five
hundred dollars will be served Chef-Boy-Ardee. Since
I really like to cook, it gives me an excuse to spend
an afternoon and evening doing something enjoy-
able and calling it charity. Everyone wins.

Usually dinner is scheduled for 7:00 P.M. So
I begin by going shopping at one or so in the afternoon. I fancy myself imitating those great chefs of
the past, not knowing what my menu will be until
I see what looks tempting and fresh at the market.
I time it so that I go right from the store to the
kitchen to begin my preparations. My goal is to have
the food cooked, the table set, the candles lit, and
the Italian music playing by 7:00 P.M. sharp. By that
time the kitchen is usually trashed, with not a con-
tainer, pan, dish, or pot unused. My apron, which
was given to me by the first person to ever win me in
a silent auction and is inscribed with the motto "Fr.
Grassi—Heavenly Food," is stained beyond belief.

Everyone is seated. I pour the wine. We begin.
I serve the meal in courses, sitting for a minute or
two to enjoy some wine with the guests. But mostly
I am on my feet until the final cup of espresso is
poured, assuring that each course has been just right.
I am also trying to move things along at a good clip
because I am tired and my feet hurt. Still, it is usually

close to midnight by the time the kitchen is cleaned and the leftovers, enough to feed another half dozen or so, are packed away in the refrigerator or in doggie bags. People do get their money's worth, as they should.

A while back one of these meals was won by someone in a raffle rather than at an auction. I did not know who she was. She telephoned me and set a date, preferring to come to the rectory for the meal. All I put on my calendar was the name "Mary" and "raffle dinner, 7:00 P.M."

I like the shopping and the early preparations best. At that point there still is no pressure. I can work at my own pace. It becomes a little like meditation to me, all by myself, focused on a single task and able to let my mind go where it chooses to go. It is profoundly relaxing. But on that day, as the afternoon progressed, like every other time, I found myself starting to watch the clock. Deadlines for certain courses had to be met or gravy would become cement and pasta would turn into paste. With ten minutes until serving time, I placed the ice cubes in the glasses and lit the candles. A compact disc of Italian hits played my father's favorite Dean Martin song, "Return to Me." Everything but me smelled great. I could relax for a few moments before the guests arrived.

Seven o'clock came and went. No problem yet. Seven fifteen. I started turning down the burners on

the stove and stirring the simmering pots a little
frantically. Seven thirty. No guests—and I realized
that I had no phone number to call. How stupid of
me. I had no way to reach this "Mary," whom I did
not know. I thought that maybe because the Chicago
Bulls were playing in the first NBA playoff game that
night, they might have forgotten. By seven forty-five
I was facing the distinct possibility of a ruined meal.
In desperation, I started calling up parishioners and
inviting them to come and eat. Those with children
had finished dinner. A few wives were waiting for
their husbands to arrive home from work. Most of
them were probably planning to sit down and watch
the basketball game. All were sympathetic but made
no commitment to join me. They said they would
see. I figured that by eight o'clock I'd wrap up and
try to save what I could. I was angry and I was hurt.

By eight fifteen, I had turned off the CD player
and had wheeled the TV set into the dining room,
where I tuned it to the Bulls game. Evidently feeling
sorry for me, three of the wives I had called sent their
husbands, and two other parishioners responded to
my voice mail as well. So we went through all eight
courses together. It wasn't until much later that
I discovered that some of them had already eaten
dinner. But that didn't stop them from eating the
cold antipasto, the hot antipasto, the salad, the pasta
with shrimp, the lamb, the roasted potatoes and

carrots, the fruit in wine with cookies, and everything else I laid out before them. And even though
the Bulls lost the game, everyone good-naturedly
stayed to clean up. They even took all the leftovers
home with them. Having gone from feeling ignored
to feeling immensely satisfied, I was at that point too
exhausted to deal with the mystery of Mary and the
other no-shows.

The mystery was solved four days later when
I listened to the messages on the church's answering
machine. Normally one of the staff goes through the
messages and relays them to the appropriate person.
But I found a message that no one had listened to. It
was from the missing Mary. And it had been recorded
the day before the dinner. A death in the family was
forcing them to postpone the meal. She apologized
and said that she would call me back eventually to
set up a new date.

So now, every time I listen to God's Word in
the Gospel parable about a wedding feast to which
no one came, I can understand a little better those
words of Jesus. All God can do is invite us to the
banquet. All God can do is offer us love. It is our
choice to accept it or make excuses. In the case of
Mary, there was a perfectly good reason to not show
up. But when I recall how bad I was feeling in my
empty kitchen, I think of how God must feel when
we choose not to accept all the infinite goodness and

total generosity that God gives us. Later we add insult to injury by shifting the blame to God for not being there for us. No wonder Jesus gave us that rousing parable about the feast and the wedding guests who rejected God. It was—and is—the lesson that God wanted us to hear loud and clear.

letting my hair grow

GROWING UP IN THE LATE SIXTIES WAS TOUGH, very tough, for many, but not for me. I enjoyed every moment of it. It was a difficult time for my parents. I tried their patience and their very faith sometimes. I was part of a generation that was very hard on our elders, who could not believe what they were seeing and hearing.

My dad didn't say very much when he saw my sideburns appear. After all, old photographs of him in his younger years showed him with fashionably long sideburns. He chose not to comment on my mustache, which followed not much later. It was only when the sideburns and the mustache met in a sort of turn-of-the-century retro handlebar that he asked me what I was doing. I don't remember my response. But he probably lifted one eyebrow in his very telling fashion and walked away with a slow shake of his head.

Mom, on the other hand, was more direct. When the mustache appeared, she blurted out a question that was really more of a demand: "So are you going to trim the mustache?" And then she would pause before adding, "off?" In my rebellion, I would just smile and let it grow longer and fuller.

It was only when my hair started to lengthen down my back and onto my shoulders that the concerns of both my parents became more evident. If you were to ask me now, a quarter of a century later, why I let it grow so long, I would have a hard time coming up with a response. I would have to dust off feelings and sentiments that have been covered over the years like the old Crosby, Stills, Nash, and Young LPs in the corner of my closet.

I know that it wasn't fashion. I never was and never will be dictated by such norms. Blessed, or cursed, with looks like mine and a body to match, it just wouldn't be worth the effort. In fact, when my oldest niece was ten and brought some of her friends to my mother's for a visit, she showed them a picture of me and said sweetly, "That's my uncle. He is a priest. He had to be one. Just look at him." Mom took her aside and said to her most earnestly that it was wrong to say such a thing, that I was still her son, and that she loved me no matter how I looked. What an interesting, backhanded compliment!

Some of my long hair was a political statement. Many who protested the Vietnam War wore long hair; it was like wearing a peace badge or carrying a placard. It guaranteed you instant entry into a community of likeminded thinkers with whom you could express your feelings without being shouted down.

Mixed in with this was a natural rebelliousness that came from many inner sources. The romantic Italian in me longed for the passion of idealism to cover me in righteousness. And those were romantic times. Part of it was a way to rebel in a gentle sort of way to the rapidly crumbling but still present structures in the seminary. Long hair wasn't in any way a theological statement. In those days the church had not yet hardened into the polarities of liberal versus conservative. My appearance was a relatively safe way (unless I was driving through Mississippi, I was told) to be a little radical without putting too much of myself on the line.

Trying to part a head of hair that ran down to my shoulders and would frizz up on humid days was no easy task. My headband kept it from getting in my eyes and blinding me when I was driving. I looked like a southern Italian Tonto, much to my father's dismay.

One day he came up with what he thought was a brilliant idea. Since, like many students, I was always hard up for cash, Dad drew me into a money-making proposal, businessman that he was. Being an immigrant who had come to this country as a teenager without a cent in his pocket, he felt I would not be a man until I was financially independent, and I had years in the seminary left before that time in my life would come.

He proposed that for every inch my sister-in-law Donna would cut from my hair, he would give me five dollars. Hearing that, my loyalty to the counterculture quickly faded. On the spot I had her clip off two inches, leaving Dad smiling and me with a crisp ten-dollar bill in the pocket of my bell-bottom jeans. But, as they say, the apple doesn't fall far from the tree. I soon learned that if I let my hair grow three more inches and then had Donna cut off two inches again, I would be an additional ten dollars richer and my hair would have an inch of its length restored. So it went. I'd grow it out four inches and have two inches cut off. Then I'd grow it out two and have one cut off. My hair was actually getting slowly longer, and I had a ready flow of spending money and no split ends.

My dad was no dummy. He never called a halt to our agreement. He kept his word even though he saw my hair getting longer. When he asked me how this could happen, I tried to feign both ignorance and innocence, and he would just smile. I think that somewhere deep inside himself he was kind of proud of my ability to make money and still have what I wanted. Maybe I wasn't just a child anymore. Or maybe it was a test to see how worldly and wise I really was and if I could stand up to the scrutiny and temptations of a society in which I was going to someday minister. I'll never know because Dad never said. I finally stopped asking for the money, and my hairstyle changed with the times.

For years, Dad continued to help me financially when I needed it. All I had to do was ask. And when I was too proud to ask, my older brothers would ask him for me. I don't know exactly when I got rid of the long hair. I still have the mustache. The beard I had for many years is gone, ever since a waitress noticed its gray and asked me if I wanted a senior discount (I was not yet fifty years old). Dad would have enjoyed the irony in that.

He was, above all, a person of his word and a person of convictions. But he never forced his beliefs on me. In his own way, he trusted me. God treats us in the same way. Since Joshua in the Old Testament, God has promised to be God for us, and we respond by haltingly saying that we will be God's people. When we are unfaithful, God is still there for us. In our feeble attempts to do better, God is there to help us. And when we stray too far away, God finds ways to entice us back by allowing God's Word to be there for us no matter how we may choose to respond at any given moment. God's Word tells us that every one of our hairs—long or short—is indeed counted, and that's very reassuring.

Stories of God's Gentleness

God's wrath and anger make for great dramatic images. Witness Cecil B. DeMille's biblical epics. But God's gentleness is so incredibly subtle that it is hard to capture and can easily be missed. A moment of safety in a speeding car could pass without us noticing God's hand in it. We can be brought to

> "Be compassionate as your Father
> is compassionate. Do not judge,
> and you will not be judged your-
> selves; do not condemn, and you
> will not be condemned yourselves;
> grant pardon, and you will be
> pardoned. Give, and there will be
> gifts for you: a full measure,
> pressed down, shaken together,
> and running over, will be poured
> into your lap; because the amount
> you measure out is the amount
> you will be given back."
>
> ~ **LUKE 6:36–38**

tears when we

encounter God's gentleness in the hands of a healing

doctor, the smile of a courageous teacher, the concern

of a caring father. In those and so many other small

and delicate ways, God's gentleness touches us,

graces us, and changes our lives forever.

love is
not blind

GENTLENESS IS NOT A QUALITY THAT MEN IN
our society actively search for or work on in their
personal lives. Why should they? Men are seldom
rewarded in the workplace for being so "incredibly
gentle." In this hypermacho environment in which
we find ourselves, even women who are in competition with men eschew such a description of themselves. It is no wonder, then, that we have developed
a cosmic lack of consciousness of God's gentleness.
For one truly cannot be gentle without having great
power. And, by definition, God is all powerful.

At first glance, my friend Denis does not
appear to be a gentle man. Not exceptionally tall, he
is still what you would call a large man—big boned,
square jawed, and solid. If you saw him and didn't
know him, the word *gentle* would not come to mind.
This ex-seminarian majored in communications in
college and became a religion teacher before marrying,

having a family, and entering the competitive business world of sales. His college interest in theater is perhaps a small hint of his gentle nature.

Denis married Beth, a woman who complements him perfectly. Like him, she is fun-loving, outgoing, honest, generous, and committed to her faith. But they are very dissimilar in other ways. Denis will offer a warm hand when one of the children is ill; he worried when one child climbed over the hill and disappeared into the waters of Lake Michigan; he dispenses more concern than aspirin. These qualities of Denis have left Beth to be the necessary pragmatic one who shows her love by letting go. It has turned out to be the right combination.

Shortly after the birth of their second child, a son, their first child was diagnosed with retinitis pigmentosa, a hereditary degenerative eye disease leading quite possibly to total blindness. It had no known cure. It began with their toddler innocently stumbling over toys on the floor. Inevitably it led to Denis and Beth having to choose to either protect their daughter from a lifetime of obstacles or free her up enough to conquer them. It would be no easy decision, and they would have to make it again and again. Many people would think that the gentle choice would be to do everything to make the world safe for her, to be easy on her and protect her.

To their credit, they made a conscious choice early on to empower their daughter to do in life whatever she would choose to do and not hold her back because of their fears or concerns. So they watched as she played T-ball, often swinging and missing, but always trying. They dealt silently with their own feelings as her coaches cheered her on for just dribbling a basketball while all the other children could sink the shot she could not make. They controlled their fears as she rode the subway with a friend to her summer job downtown. They did what all good parents want to do for their children. And in so doing, they were able to help her develop into the fine young woman she is today.

Over the years, as Coleen's eyesight has deteriorated, her love of music and her talent to play and sing it has grown almost exponentially. Early on, her acute hearing and a sensitivity to what certain sounds communicated were evident. Once when she was a child, she began to cry as her parents were having a discussion, albeit a heated one. When they turned to her and asked her what was wrong, she blurted out, "Daddy, please don't hurt Mommy!" Gentle Denis, who never would have touched his wife in anger, realized at that moment how strong and intimidating his acting-trained voice could be. It would never happen again.

Being a successful businessman meant that Denis traveled a lot. But he made sure that he would always be present for his daughter. And this is what true gentleness is all about. Coleen grew interested in musical comedy. With her talent for singing and the fact that she could memorize the set of the stage and feel comfortable and secure with her movements, she was given roles in a number of community-theater productions. In a world where some fathers coach their child's baseball teams and the phrase "soccer moms" has entered into our vocabulary, Denis found a way to uniquely support and be with his daughter while she was involved with something she truly loved to do.

So, picture if you will this bear of a man, not at all unfamiliar with the stage, trading in his three-piece business suit for a costume and giving his daughter the precious gift of his time and presence at rehearsals and performances. There he would be, in the background, nothing more than an extra, perhaps a servant in *The King and I*, while Coleen sang and performed and grew into the capable and secure person she has become. Did he look foolish? We know the answer to that. Did it stretch his schedule? Certainly. A cell phone has no place at a rehearsal or during a performance. Did his coworkers and bosses fully comprehend the importance of what he was doing? Are you kidding? Not in this competitive world. For too many of us, the only option we would have come up with would have been to show up for a performance, cheer her on from the audience, and be content with that. Denis needed and wanted to do more.

None of his actions will be able to restore Coleen's eyesight. Nothing he or Beth can do will keep their daughter from moments of pain or loneliness or anger, all of which she now writes about eloquently. He cannot possibly protect her from what life offers her. No parents do that for any child, no matter how much they want to or how much they love their child. But somehow Denis and Beth continue to find the right balance, ways of being there for and with Coleen that are caring but never smothering, helpful but not overpowering. In short, they are gentle and loving and challenging.

In similar ways, God's gentleness envelops us. No doubt we will stumble, stub our toes, and sometimes be incredibly hurt by what happens in our lives. Too often we question why God would allow such things to happen—a question that really cannot be answered. We keep ourselves from understanding and feeling God's loving presence within us. But no matter how the world or life or even God looks to us at the moment, we need to realize and be open to the incredible gentleness that God shows us time and time again, a gentleness strong enough to help us be the person we can be.

in defense of crying

ONCE I WROTE A REFLECTION ABOUT JESUS
laughing. I think I made a good case for it. I'm
sure Jesus cried too—over Jerusalem, his family, his
friends, Judas. Thinking about Jesus crying makes
some folks uncomfortable. To me it reflects the gentleness of God, who loves us enough to cry over us.
I realized this one Sunday morning after Mass.

I stood there, silently amazed, listening to
ninety-year-old Anne, shrunken by not only her
years but also the many burdens they represented.
Of her three children, she had already buried two.
If life were fair, no mother would ever have to
endure the pain of burying a child. To do so twice
is somehow more than doubly tragic and, ultimately,
haunting.

For whatever reason, Anne was telling those
who were standing around her about her deceased
daughter's illness. Just shortly before her death, her

daughter inexplicably insisted that her mother promise not to cry when the daughter died. How unfair of her. No one, not even a dying child, has the right or privilege to ask a parent not to grieve such a profound loss. But Anne made that promise and kept it and now was sharing its burden with us. I told her quite plainly that it was not a promise that I felt she had to keep. If she so desired or needed to cry, she should do it.

She looked at me as if she were looking at a stranger and not her pastor. "You don't understand," she said. "I told you I haven't cried and now I can't, even if I wanted to." She looked around the church almost wistfully. Clearly she was still haunted.

I have to admit that it is very hard for me to grasp that people can control their crying. I cry easily. It is, I am sure, the Italian in me. And I have great role models in my mother and father, who always seemed to cry at the right times, not just with reckless abandon. Tears for us, be they of great joy or anger or sadness, were a clear sign of the depth of love present in our relationships. I have grown to respect tears as monitors of that love. It all goes well beyond some sappy exhortation of everlasting love on a Valentine's Day card. Tears can and do communicate, without any spoken words, the real love that is present.

Having admitted all this, I must also confess that there are still times when my crying comes from someplace deep inside of me and takes me completely by surprise. And this occurred on that very day when Anne told us about her inability to cry.

Anne said these things just before Mass began. After that same Mass, I waited quietly on the first steps of the church to greet the parishioners. Since another priest was celebrating the service, I positioned myself on the steps of the church just as communion had begun. I was all by myself. Up the street, children and parents were coming out of the school. The religious-education classes had just been dismissed. A familiar mother and son pair came walking toward me. I recognized Andy instantly. His ready smile and wave were always a welcome sight. Despite having Down's syndrome, he was doing well enough in his religious-education class to be able to make his First Holy Communion this year. It was only a few months away.

Andy came running up to me. He used to get a real kick out of rubbing my beard with his hand and was clearly disappointed after I shaved it off. So now he is content to just gently touch my mustache. It makes him laugh the glorious laugh of the innocent. On this day my eyes caught his in a particular way as they sparkled happily, and I saw that innocence and peace in them.

Before I knew it, I was carried back in my mind to a long-past Taste of Chicago food festival on the city's lakefront. There, along with my good friend and brother priest Jim Noone, I was surrounded by literally hundreds of thousands of people happily eating and drinking their way from one restaurant booth to another. As I was about to make a headlong dash toward the barbecued turkey legs, Jim suddenly stopped. "We've got to help him," he said.

"Who?" I asked impatiently.

"Don't you see him? He's right in front of us. He's one of God's special friends, and I am sure he is lost."

I looked around and saw only face after face of revelers. I could see nothing unusual until Jim walked right up to one of those faces, one I confess I would have walked right by without noticing anything wrong. Jim asked him if he was alright. The young man shouted in a loud, scared, and distressed voice, "My mother's lost!"

In a soothing voice Jim asked him, "What does she look like?"

"She's a girl, and she's wearing a dress!" was the total description given.

Jim told him not to worry and that he would stay with him until his mother came back. I was just about to go for the police when, fortunately, she appeared, equally distraught until she saw her son's smiling face buried in a cinnamon roll Jim had bought him. She thanked us as they walked off together.

Jim had a profound love for those he called "God's special friends." And they returned that love to him unconditionally. It was a delight to behold. Jim ultimately developed an entire parish ministry he called God's Special Friends that touched many hearts. I was thinking about Jim as Andy put his hand in mine and said, "Jesus. Communion." Then I started to cry. Jim's death, almost a decade ago, had come too soon. I missed him, his friendship, his priesthood. I gave Andy a big hug, realizing that had it not been for Jim, I would most certainly not have noticed the specialness in Andy.

That Sunday, the many announcements to be read and the lengthy closing hymn gave me the time I needed for what my mother would have called "a really good cry." I cried for Jim in sadness and I cried in joy for special Andy. Could anyone be worthier to share in the body and blood of Jesus? I doubt it. I cried for Anne, who was unable to cry for her daughter. And while I was at it, I cried for her daughter as well. Indeed, it was a very good cry.

But I barely had the time to wipe my eyes dry and give my nose a healthy blow. Like Moses coming down the mountain, people were descending the church steps. *Do they cry?* I wondered. *Do they know God has cried for them?* I noticed Anne grabbing the rail a little unsteadily. I took her hand and helped her down the stairs. She turned her head to nod a polite thank you. I think I genuinely surprised her with my kiss, another Italian instinct. With her fading hearing, I'm sure she didn't hear me say gently, "This is from your daughter, from Andy, and from me." I might have seen a tear form in the corner of her eye. But then again, maybe it was just me starting up all over again as I prayed, "Gentle God, be with her."

hero--of the unsung variety

LET ME TELL YOU ABOUT SOMEONE WHO, IN A
time when we have lost all idea of what courage and
love and dedication and gentleness mean, is a true
hero. It is a privilege for me to relate his story so that
it will not be lost, but celebrated.

I first met him on the front steps of the church.
He always had a wide smile on his face and a warm
greeting for me. Usually he came alone. On occasion
an adult daughter, who inherited his open and honest
smile, accompanied him. And, on very rare occasions,
he would be pushing his wife in front of him in her
wheelchair. She had multiple sclerosis. If memory
serves me, there were only a handful of times that
she was strong enough to come and worship with
him. His name was Norb.

It's hard for me to believe that for more than
a decade this was the extent of our weekly contact.
Sometimes I noticed behind his smile a wince that

was a result of his painful bad back. But he never complained about it. If anyone had asked me about him, I would have told him or her all that I really knew—that he was a good and decent man.

Norb's wife died recently. She had been in and out of the hospital as her disease progressed. Even after the doctors were forced to place a feeding tube in her stomach, Norb still held out in hope for her return home. Norb came very close to having his wish come true when the pneumonia that had complicated his wife's condition somehow passed. To everyone's surprise, she was able to eat again. The doctor scheduled a date for her release from the hospital. But while watching television in her hospital bed, she quietly looked away and breathed her last breath.

As I sat in the undertaker's office listening to this gentle man talk about his wife and the rich life they had lived together, I began to realize that I was in the presence of someone truly special. At one point in a story he was telling, he referred to someone calling him "Teach." I asked if indeed he was a teacher. I never would have guessed that he had been a high school and college mathematics teacher who had traveled more than fifty miles a day to his school and had coached football and basketball. He had continued to do all of this as long as he could after his wife was diagnosed with MS. Finally, he freely gave up the profession he loved so much to take care of the woman he loved even more.

He told me about how he had worked for his degrees on a G.I. loan after the Korean War and how he very much wanted to use his skills as a volunteer in our parish grammar school. His wife, in fact, had encouraged him to do so even though they both knew in reality that she needed his constant care. So he rightly and unselfishly decided not to leave her side. He was somewhat comforted that she died in the hospital. If he had taken her home and she had died there, he would have blamed himself for doing something wrong.

At the wake, his love for her was unmistakable. His faith assured him that she was no longer in any pain. But he also knew that his life would be changing dramatically now that she was gone. Already his heart could not stop missing her greatly. I said the traditional prayers. When I shook his hand, that familiar smile returned to his face. He told me that he was pleased that I would be celebrating the liturgy the next day. I knew that the faith that had sustained him through the years would get him through his loss.

As we left the funeral home, one of the undertakers, a lifelong parishioner, reflected on the fact that the man was a person who had taken the phrase "in sickness and in health, until death do us part" seriously. She then told me about how the couple had traveled all over the country, him pushing the wheelchair so that they could see everything together. It was another sign of the courage and the love that they shared. He never complained, the undertaker said, about what had befallen the two of them, even when it meant changing and adapting his own life so dramatically.

I was glad I had chosen to attend the wake. It was my scheduled day off, and the associate pastor would have covered it for me. Since I would be celebrating the funeral Mass, I would have fulfilled my obligation to the family then. But how could I not pay my respects to someone who had given me that gentle smile week after week? In return, I was able to learn more about him than I would have otherwise. What a great gift, what a grace had been given to me by God! I came home from the wake and immediately wrote this reflection to honor "Teach" and his wife and their love for each other, gentle yet strong enough to transcend all physical limitations.

"Teach" may not realize it, but long after he gave up his classroom, he continues to be a teacher. His commitment to his wife and the simplicity of his choosing without regret to live life fully challenges all of us to look at our own lives with much greater honesty. We need to ask ourselves if we are fulfilling without any excuses or complaints the commitments that we made. Anyone privileged to know "Teach" cannot help but learn from him. His living out the gospel of Jesus is neither too esoteric nor beyond our capabilities. His very ordinary manner is what ultimately makes him so special.

Many more such gentle heroes are all around us. They are good and simple people who, without fanfare or headlines, quietly take what life has given them and live honest, compassionate, courageous, and loving lives. They do it not because they have to, but because they freely choose to do so. They are the heroes. And they are the saints. We need to acknowledge them and we need to honor them because they reflect God's gentle love for us. "Teach" is one of them. And so I lift him up with these few inadequate words.

the
healer

I HATE NOT FEELING WELL AND BEING SICK.
Some seasons, when the influenza is particularly vir-
ulent, the anticipation of catching it is as bad as the
bug. When it hits, I cover myself with a soft, down-
filled comforter that I received as a Christmas gift. I
shudder with the chills and, most of all, feel sorry for
myself. It seems that no matter how "comforting"
the covering is, I still miss that wonderful feeling of
being tucked in by my mother, with her cool hand
wiping my fevered brow. I long for the homemade
chicken broth with pastina and the fresh-squeezed
orange juice she would have ready at my bedside.

If I had a fever, she would automatically call the
family doctor. Dr. Del Chicca was a wonderful, gray-
haired, mustached patrician of a man. Initially he
practiced medicine in a well-to-do area of Philadelphia.
But then he found himself chosen, as the story went,
specifically by Mother (and later, Saint) Francis

Xavier Cabrini, to come to Chicago and work with the growing number of Italian immigrants crowding the hospitals that she had just opened and staffed with her Missionary Sisters of the Sacred Heart. He came; I guess no one turns down a saint. That must be what makes someone a saint.

Dr. Del Chicca would always appear the same day Mom called him. Not only did he make house calls, he would even make them on a Wednesday, which was traditionally a doctor's day off, and on weekends. Often he would arrive early in the morning or late in the evening, depending on his busy schedule. But he would always be there for us.

Three things stand out in my mind about his visits. First of all, when Mom talked to him, her Italian would switch from the familiar southern hill dialect that we always heard around the house to perfect Italian. It was a noticeable difference. Their conversation was warm and polite, and reinforced, to me, what a gentleman he was. After all, our household was not used to modulated voices and controlled gestures.

Second, Mom would pay him five dollars for the visit, ten if it included a penicillin shot. But before he left, he'd come back into the bedroom and quietly slip me the money my mom had just given him. It made getting sick and having to endure a shot bearable—well, almost.

But what I remember most about Dr. Del Chicca is how incredibly warm and gentle his hands were. Sometimes his stethoscope would be cold when he placed it on my chest or on my back. But his warm hands were always gentle and healing, never rough or indifferent. I felt better and safe. I knew that everything was going to be just fine.

Over the years I grew to appreciate the genuine affection that Dr. Del Chicca had for our family. My sister's death from polio shortly before my birth was traumatic for him. While he was unable to save my sister, he promised my mother during her difficult pregnancy with me just months after my sister's death that I would be born normal and healthy. And so it seemed that I always remained special to him. Perhaps I became the son he never had. Later in life, I came to learn that more than a few times his healing extended beyond the physical when he dealt with my family. His counsel proved more valuable to both my parents on a number of occasions.

After I was ordained, to my embarrassment, Dr. Del Chicca would make a point to see me ahead of the other patients waiting in his office, who had been there a good deal earlier than I had been. After my exam he would lecture me about the struggle in the world between good and evil and how I as a priest should confront it. This would cause many of the other patients, who had been waiting for my visit with him to end, to develop severe hypertension. I could tell by their looks as I was leaving his office that they were wishing on me maladies that even good Dr. Del Chicca could not cure. No matter; I always felt wonderful after being with him, regardless of what had been ailing me.

Eventually the doctor and his wife retired to a comfortable villa in Italy. That had been his dream. But the rampant corruption they faced there and the fact that too many people took advantage of his generosity and concern forced them to return reluctantly to America. Saddened and disillusioned, he wanted no one to know of his fate. Inevitably, he fell sick.

Mom heard of what happened and visited him in the hospital. She was the only former patient he allowed to visit him. When she realized that he was dying, she called me. I immediately went to see him. It was a special grace for me. We talked for hours.

I listened as this good and gentle healer of body and soul reflected on his life and his personal shortcomings. When he was finished, he asked me for absolution. It was a humbling moment for me. He reached out his hands and placed them in mine. They were warm, like I remembered them to be. I just quietly held on to him for I don't know how long, thinking of the thousands of healing touches that he had given to so many frightened and hurting people, most of them simple, humble immigrants and their families. I was in the presence of a true healer.

Though he knew bishops and cardinals, his widow told me that he had asked that I celebrate his funeral Mass. In the chapel of Columbus Hospital in Chicago, at the altar containing a relic of St. Francis Xavier Cabrini, who built that institution and eventually died there, I spoke to and prayed with hundreds of people, most of them in the medical profession. But seated in their midst were my parents, grateful symbols of those immigrants to whom he had dedicated his life.

At the end of the Mass, I invited everyone to look up at the mural on the ceiling of the chapel. Painted many decades earlier, it included the figure of a young, mustached immigrant standing tall, with a hopeful look on his face. Dr. Del Chicca had been used as the model.

It is through such special people that we feel God's healing and gentle touch. So, more than once since his death, I have found my way back to that chapel. I've gone there when I needed healing in my life. I look up and see that figure of Dr. Del Chicca and I feel his—and God's—warm touch, and I am instantly better.

angels
and buicks

IT WAS A SILLY LITTLE ORNAMENT I RECEIVED as a Christmas present. The woman who gave it to me I had known for years. I had taught her son in high school more than two decades ago. Once again, years later, our paths had crossed. Cardboard, paper, and glitter had been fashioned into a not-so-cute little angel with floppy wings and a kind of Robin Hood cap. It was holding onto a plastic wheel or tire. In one of its hands was a small scroll that read, "Don't drive faster than your guardian angel can fly." It made no sense to hang it on my Christmas tree, so I hung it from the rearview mirror of my car for no other reason than just to have something hanging there. I doubted that it would have any effect on my driving, and it didn't. I knew that angels had become all the rage. But for me this was nothing more than an ornament to hang on my car's mirror.

Sometime later, I was scheduled to visit some friends for dinner across the city on a Saturday night. I don't much like the drive across town on the expressways on a Saturday night. It seems that more crazy drivers are on the highways all the time. Still, it never really bothered me before. But for some reason the whole week prior to the scheduled dinner I found myself thinking about the drive and dreading it, almost to the point of calling and canceling. Such thoughts embarrassed me and made me feel that I was turning into an old man way before my time. So I let my feelings pass and didn't change my plans.

Saturday came and I drove to my friend's home without incident. We shared a wonderful evening of conversation, support, and down-home southern cooking. Being with good friends is one of life's mellowest graces. The time went quickly. When I looked at my watch, it was after midnight. I'd stayed much later than I had expected and certainly later than my hosts had anticipated.

I realized that it was going to be a long drive home through some pretty rough traffic. I put on a tape of wonderful gospel music so I could sing along and stay awake. I knew that it would keep me relaxed as I headed back home. My worst fears about the traffic were not realized. The roads were clear and traffic moved along quickly. Soon I was lost in the soaring harmonies and in the freedom of driving with the windows rolled down and the sunroof wide open.

Out of habit, I glanced down at my speedometer and was mildly surprised to see the needle at about eighty-five miles per hour. And I was at a place where the speed limit was dropping from fifty-five to forty-five. State police are often ready and waiting for speeders in these areas. I started to brake.

Something happened at that precise moment. I looked at the speedometer. I braked. And that is when I noticed a car stalled no more than twenty feet in front of me. It must have been there for a while, since its flashing emergency lights were beginning to slow and fade as the battery wore down. That must have been why I hadn't seen it from farther down the road.

No one was in the car. I was so close to it that I could tell that it was an old, beat-up Plymouth Reliant station wagon with more rust than paint coloring it. In a split second, my mind calculated that even though I was braking, I would still back-end the stalled car in just a matter of seconds. I thought of swerving into an adjacent lane, but I knew that with all the traffic around me I would probably sideswipe someone else and possibly cause a chain-reaction accident. In that same split second I remembered that my car had airbags, that I was wearing a seat belt, and that unless there was an explosion or another car hit me from behind, I had a chance, if even a slim one, of surviving. I closed my eyes. Or did I? I braced myself for the impact.

But my car swerved into the lane on my left, just missing the stalled vehicle. My car then cut back all the way over to the lane on the far right. I was expecting to be hit by someone. It never happened. I looked into the mirror, and the headlights of the nearest cars were a good ten car lengths behind me. It was as though a buffer zone of some kind had been created around me.

I expected my adrenaline to kick in, my heart to start beating in my chest, and the combination of fear and relief to take over my body. None of those things happened. I was perfectly relaxed. I was stunned. All I knew for sure was that I never could have moved quickly enough to get around the stalled car. My reflexes couldn't have responded so accurately. I began to feel incredibly safe and secure as I drove on.

The gospel music on the tape kept playing. Each song became a joyous anthem to God's saving power. I began thinking about why there had been no crash. I looked into the rearview mirror, and my eye caught the angel ornament bobbing and moving around. It got me to thinking. Maybe God was gently trying to tell me something just now. But what? I remembered all the stories about guardian angels we had been told in school. I was resisting buying into the New Age rage that angels had become. But I had to admit that something had just happened over which I had no control at all. So for the rest of the trip home I debated with myself. No, I would not call it a coincidence. I refused to cheapen what had happened and turn it into chance. Divine intervention? That thought kind of scared me because I would then have to add to it the question Why? Perhaps it could be that my two good friends who were deceased were looking out for me from heaven. That was a little more palatable, but no more plausible. I decided that I could simply live with it, if I decided not to tell anyone about it.

I pulled the car into the garage, locked it, and went up to my room. It was late and I was tired and I didn't want to think about it anymore. I just felt grateful. The next morning, when I unlocked the door of my car, I noticed something on the passenger-side seat. It was a little strip of white paper. I picked it up and turned it over. It read, "Don't drive faster than your guardian angel can fly." I looked at the ornament. It was still hanging from the mirror, but empty-handed. When had the paper fallen from its hands? I hadn't noticed it when I left the car the night before. But I had been tired and in a hurry to go to bed. I could have missed it. But then again . . .

I sold that car a few years later and got a good price for it, ten years old and no dents. It never was in an accident. The ornament? It's a little dusty and a little faded, but you better believe it's hanging on the rearview mirror of my new car. And I am finally able to share my story, not at all embarrassed to say that there are inexplicable times when we are held gently in the palms of God's hands.

afterword

I LOOK BACK OVER THIS NEW BATCH OF STORIES
and realize how incredibly blessed and graced my
life has been. It is not fashionable these days to say
how much you love your ministry. But the very
uncertainty that frightens some away from it is what
excites and challenges me. I am offered a smorgas-
bord of people and situations every day, and I will
continue to eat it all up until I am beyond full.

I realize that from these stories and the images
of my family, friends, and parishioners that I share,
the mosaic that is my life begins to form an image.
What you see is me. I make no apology for who I
am, what I have done, and how I got to this point
in my life. As I read these stories, gathered together,
what I see is God's hand clearly taking me where
God wants me—with all my limitations and flaws—
to go.

The journey so far has given me a much
greater appreciation of the stories of faith that make
up sacred Scripture and the stories of the people of
faith that I bump into almost every day. So often
after a talk or a reading people will share with me

stories of their youth or struggles or encounters with God. At precisely those moments I feel that I am quite blessed.

As I put the pen down for this volume (and yes, I still write it all out longhand on legal pads) I find myself looking forward to whatever stories today and tomorrow will bring. Even if I am never blessed to be able to share them, the fact that they have happened and are mine will be gift enough from God.

So I invite you to take this slim volume with you or leave it behind, to go confidently to your own stories. Experience all life has to offer, especially the simple and mundane ways in which God's presence will be there for you. Enjoy every minute of every story that awaits you.

REV. DOMINIC J. GRASSI uses his experience as both a pastor of a growing urban parish and an author to extend his ministry. He hosts retreats for clergy, both deacons and priests, throughout the country. He offers Lenten missions and individual talks centered on sharing personal stories of bumping into God. Grassi also conducts small group workshops on storytelling. He shows teachers, school administrators, and those working in religious education programs how to tie individual stories and experiences to the greater story of faith. In addition, he facilitates parish staff days of reflection. In all that he does, his approach is pastoral; and his stories are central to the presentation.

While Grassi's time is limited because of his pastoral responsibilities, he is available to speak on a limited basis. If you are interested in having him present to your group, you can reach him at *domgrassi@aol.com.*